Kids Review Kids' Books

375 Reviews of Favorite Books That Get Children to Read and Read and Read!

Compiled by the Editors of  Magazine

SCHOLASTIC
PROFESSIONAL BOOKS

New York ▼ Toronto ▼ London ▼ Auckland ▼ Sydney

Thanks to all the kids who contributed their
great reviews. Maybe we'll be reading novels
and nonfiction books by you someday!

—The Editors

Scholastic Inc. grants purchasers permission to photocopy these reviews for classroom use.
No other part of this publication may be reproduced in whole or in part, or stored in a
retrieval system, or transmitted in any form or by any means, electronic, mechanical, photo-
copying, recording, or otherwise, without written permission of the publisher. For information regarding permission, write to Scholastic Inc., 555 Broadway, New York, NY 10012.

Cover and interior design by Ellen Matlach Hassell
for Boultinghouse & Boultinghouse, Inc.

Cover art by Laura Cornell

ISBN 0-590-60346-9

Printed in the U.S.A.

12 11 10 9 8 7 6 5 4 3 2 1   7 8 9 / 00 / 01 / 02

Contents

Introduction

Dear Reader,

Books are magical. They help us imagine other lives and other lands, dream impossible dreams, and envision the person we want to become. Books let us swim with the sharks, rocket through the galaxies, and walk among giants. When I finish reading a good book, I can't wait to talk about it. Talking about a book allows me to linger in its spell a little longer. I want to tell everyone about the book, what it meant to me, why I liked it, and why I think they'll like it.

Kids like to talk about books, too. And that's exactly what they do in **Kids Review Kids' Books**. They talk about all kinds of books—from time-honored classics to the latest best-sellers. They talk about the good parts, the scary parts, the laugh-out-loud parts, the parts that amazed them, and the parts that grossed them out. In short, they talk about the parts that will make other kids want to drop everything, dash to the nearest library, and READ.

The enthusiasm of these young critics is contagious: "You'll never believe how cool this book I read is!" exclaims a fourth-grader in one review. "This book . . . is so spectacular that you won't stop reading, even for a day at the ballpark!" raves a sixth-grader in another. The books included here are as diverse as the kids who reviewed them, but there's one thing they all have in common: They're books kids want to read. **Kids Review Kids' Books** reflects the results of a national survey in which kids reviewed their favorite books. More than 10,000 kids submitted reviews; their top choices are presented here.

Kids Review Kids' Books is a useful reference for kids and adults alike. Young readers can flip through the listings to find recommended reading for whatever suits their fancy at a given moment—something spooky, something serious, something silly. They can find a book on a topic that interests them, or a book by a favorite author. They can preview a book they plan to read or compare notes with a reviewer on a book they've just finished. Adults can browse through these "field-tested" selections for tips about books suited to their young readers' particular tastes.

In these reviews, kids show that they are discerning critics. Their styles vary. Some reviewers like to keep you guessing about the outcome of a book, while others lay it on the line. All of them offer juicy tidbits and fantastic facts to delight potential readers.

These reviewers know you don't just read a good book; you feel it. Your spine tingles, your stomach flips, your brain buzzes, your side splits with laughter. They know about the magic. And through their reviews, kids pass that magic along to other readers by sharing the inside scoop—the secrets, the mysteries, the surprises—contained within the covers of a favorite book.

The passion kids have for reading is abundantly evident in the voices of these reviewers. They have the power to start a reading epidemic. We hope kids will turn to the pages of **Kids Review Kids' Books** again and again—for information, for insights, for fun—and that they'll rise to the challenge presented by one young critic: "Read this book....Take the chance."

Cordially,

Bernice E. Cullinan
Professor of Reading,
New York University

How to Use This Book

Who knows what stories make kids fall off their seats laughing? What books keep them reading under the covers with flashlights, long after the final bedtime warning? Other kids know, that's who!

That's what Scholastic was thinking when we sponsored our recent Storyworks Book Review Contest. What we didn't know was that more than 10,000 kids—from Los Angeles, California, to Little Rock, Arkansas—would flood us with memorable submissions. It took some doing to whittle down that pile of great reviews to a manageable number, but somehow we succeeded.

So without further ado—on with the book! On the pages that follow, you'll find 375 reviews of books on a range of topics wider than the Grand Canyon. How do you decide which one is right for you? Here are some tips for using *Kids Review Kids' Books* to pick titles that will keep you turning pages.

Title The title gives you a clue about the book's topic. If you know the title, use the Title Index on page 203 to find out the author.

Pages How long is the book? Can you read it in an afternoon, or do you want to save it for your vacation?

Author One of the most important details of a book review—who wrote it! The books here are listed alphabetically by author. If you like one book, you'll definitely want to check out others by the same author.

Extra! Look for extra tidbits about the review. You'll learn more about the authors, other books, and fun facts about the topic that might stir your interest in the books.

Genre These flags will tell you what type of book it is. Is it a mystery or a biography? Knowing the genre will help you decide if the book will interest you. Refer to the list on pages 8 and 9 to learn what the flags mean.

Reviewer Our reviewers are kids, just like you are. You might or might not agree with their reviews. If you don't, perhaps you'll want to write your own reviews (see page 200 for some tips). (Don't forget to look at the reviewer's grade level to see if the book he or she read will be on target for you.)

Little House in the Big Woods

by Laura Ingalls Wilder

238 pages

BIOGRAPHY

FRIENDSHIP & FAMILY

HISTORY

Little House in the Big Woods is written by Laura Ingalls Wilder. This is about Laura Ingalls Wilder as a child and how she lived with her family. She lived about 100 years ago. I liked this book because it made me feel like I was really there. This book reminds me of my mother when she tells me about her life as a child. I liked Laura because she was always happy. I recommend this book to kids that like true stories from the past.

—Jamie Cherry, Grade 4
Kenner, Louisiana

A Late Start to a Big Success

Laura Ingalls Wilder's books describe her pioneer life from 1870 to 1894. But she didn't write the first book until 1932, when she was 65! Her daughter, Rose Wilder Lane, helped her shape childhood memories into exciting stories, spiced with details of everyday homesteading life. For a different true account of a pioneer girlhood, try *Caddie Woodlawn* and its sequel *Magical Melons* by Carol Ryrie Brink.

A Note About Literary Genres

Have you ever browsed through your library looking for a book to take home and read? How do you decide which books to pull off the shelves? Sometimes librarians put stickers on the spines to give you clues about the books' topics. They might have a lightbulb symbol for science or a question mark for mysteries, so that you can tell a book's genre. A genre is a category of literature. Look at the list below. You can see the genre of some of the books reviewed in this collection. What is your favorite genre? Flip through and look for these flags to find the books you're sure to enjoy.

 Stories of brave deeds and thrilling escapades

 Horses, cats, and wild animals wag these "tales"

 True stories of real people who achieve greatness

 Inspiring stories of people who maintain their spirit while overcoming life's difficulties

 Inspiring stories of people dealing with hardships and facing their emotions

 Science, nature, and the world around you are central to the characters in these stories

 Imagination takes the reader to faraway, fantastic places where animals talk and dreams come true

 **FRIENDSHIP & FAMILY** — The characters in these stories prove the value of friendship, loyalty, and caring for others

 **HISTORY** — These stories are true or are based on events that really happened

 **HUMOR** — These stories are created to make you laugh out loud

 **MULTICULTURAL** — Get to know a variety of cultures and explore different worlds through these stories

 **MYSTERY** — Can you solve these whodunits before the hero does?

 **POETRY** — Words carefully chosen to evoke feelings and for the beauty of their sound

 **SCIENCE FICTION** — Take a leap into the future and look at what the world might be like one day

 **SPORTS** — True stories or fiction based on the world of home runs, jump shots, gymnastics, and personal challenges

 **THRILLS & CHILLS** — These spooky stories will keep you on the edge of your seat

Reviews

Borreguita and the Coyote

by Verna Aardema

40 pages

ANIMAL

FANTASY & FOLKLORE

MULTICULTURAL

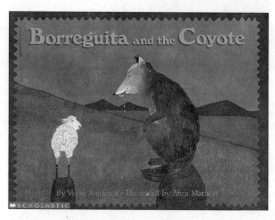

This has to be the best book I read this year! *Borreguita and the Coyote* is a tale from Ayutla, Mexico, retold by Verna Aardema. It is about a Borreguita, which means "little lamb" in Spanish, and a coyote that wants to eat her. What is Borreguita to do but trick coyote time and time again? Borreguita is too smart to be caught and eaten by coyote. The last trick is the best because coyote never comes back. Everyone should read this book because it has great pictures and it also teaches you a few Spanish words.

Danny H. Tarango, Grade 2
El Paso, Texas

Song and Dance Man

by Karen Ackerman

32 pages

FRIENDSHIP & FAMILY

HUMOR

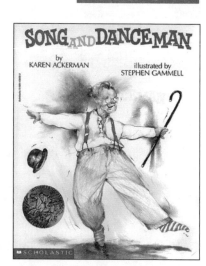

This story is about a grandfather who liked showing his grandchildren how it used to be in the good old days when he danced on the vaudeville stage. He takes his grandchildren up to the attic, and he finds his tap shoes, hats, vests, and bowties. His grandchildren try on his hats. Then grandfather dances for them. If you want to know what it was like before television, as I did, read this great book.

Meredith LaSala, Grade 4
Sarasota, Florida

The Gold Coin

by Alma F. Ada

32 pages

FANTASY & FOLKLORE

MULTICULTURAL

The Gold Coin is about Juan, a man who has been a thief for a long time. One day, he sees Doña Josefa holding a gold coin. He decides he wants to steal it and follows her everywhere. When he finally catches up with her, she gives him the gold coin. But he gives it back. Now he knows what's more valuable than taking. It is giving.

I think this is a very good book for children. It teaches a lesson about not stealing and about giving.

Krystal Davis, Grade 4
Woodinville, Washington

Cam Jansen and the Mystery of the Monster Movie

by David A. Adler

64 pages

MYSTERY

The story is about a fifth-grade girl called Cam Jansen. She's called Cam because she says "click" when she uses her photographic memory, just like a camera. One day, Cam, her friend Eric Shelton, and her parents are enjoying a movie when suddenly the screen goes dark. The second reel of the film is missing! Now Cam, Eric, and Cam's mother have to solve the mystery, using clues they find, so that they can see the rest of the movie.

Reading this book made me feel happy and excited. All through the book, Cam used her memory and her smartness to find out what she wanted to know.

I learned from this book that if I put my mind to it, I can accomplish anything. I recommend this book to people who like mysteries.

This story is like many other Cam Jansen books, such as *Cam Jansen and the Mystery of the U.F.O.* All Cam Jansen books are about her adventures using her photographic memory, and I wouldn't change anything about this book or any others. I like them just the way they are.

James Marotta, Grade 3
Wantagh, New York

Picture This!

Do you have a photographic memory like Cam Jansen's? You might if you're a child, but it usually disappears with age. Here's a simple test. Look at a picture with lots of details for 30 seconds. Then look at a blank piece of paper. Can you still "see" details in the picture?

Martin Luther King, Jr.: Free at Last

by David A. Adler

BIOGRAPHY

CHALLENGE/ COURAGE

HISTORY

I was sad when Martin's best friend said, "You can't play because you are black." I understand how he felt when he never got to play with his best friends again. I'm glad that he taught black and white people to get along. He made the world a better place!

**Peter Franklin, Grade 2
Houston, Texas**

Separate, but Not Equal

When Martin Luther King, Jr., was young, southern states had Jim Crow laws. These laws called for separate facilities for blacks. Blacks had to drink from different water fountains, go to different schools, and sit in the back of the bus. Not only were the facilities for African-Americans separate, they were usually inferior.

Meet Samantha

by Susan S. Adler

CHALLENGE/ COURAGE

FRIENDSHIP & FAMILY

HISTORY

This story is about Samantha Parkington, who lived with her grandmother. Samantha's mother and father died in a boating accident when she was five. Samantha got along very well with her grandmother's servant, whose name was Nellie. She was a very caring and considerate child. At first everything was good, but then her friends Jessie and Nellie had to leave. Her world was falling apart. She learned a valuable lesson in this book, that "actions speak louder than words." She put this lesson into practice by giving her doll she loved very much to Nellie.

This book was very enjoyable. I liked it because I learned how a girl my age lived back in 1904. Samantha lived with a rich family, and Nellie was a servant. They were both nine and lived totally different lives.

Krista Bowman, Grade 4 ·······
Cumberland, Maryland

Teeth Week

by Nancy Alberts

80 pages

Do you like books about problems? I do. That's why I think everyone should read *Teeth Week*. Everyone in Liza's class lost at least one tooth, but not Liza. NOT ONE! And now that it's Teeth Week at her school, everyone is making fun of her. Even the bully in her class is making fun of her, making her feel left out, like a baby. Liza wants to lose her first tooth now, but she doesn't know how! I think everyone will relate to this book. I can. I was also the only one with all my baby teeth. Enjoy!

**Colleen Koester, Grade 4
Columbus, Ohio**

You're Diphyodont!

Humans are *diphyodont* (DE-Fie-a-dawnt). In other words, they have two sets of teeth: baby teeth and permanent teeth. Most kids lose their first tooth (usually one of the bottom front ones, or *incisors*) between the ages of five and seven. The bottom, or root, dissolves, and the top, or crown, falls out.

Little Women

by Louisa May Alcott

336 pages

Little Women is a wonderful book. It is all about four girls who are growing up: Jo, an energetic girl with a continually growing anger; Meg, a sensible beauty; Beth, an ever-loving and peaceful girl; and Amy who is very artistic.

These four girls go through many sad moments, such as Beth's dreadful sickness, their father's illness, and Amy's punishment in school. But they also have happy times, like Jo's writing success, Meg's first dance, and Beth's wonderful piano playing. The only way these girls made it through the hard times was by their love for each other and their parents' love. I recommend this book to any girl who loves well-written books; this certainly is one. Jo would say it's "a jolly good story!" This book is so well written, I actually felt sad at sad times, happy at happy times, mad at mad times, etc. My favorite character in this book is Jo, for she is always full of energy. This book has no artwork.

If you like this book, you'll like the sequel, *Little Men*, also.

**Laura Bassett, Grade 4
Quakertown, Pennsylvania**

Little Women

by Louisa May Alcott

336 pages

CHALLENGE/
COURAGE

FRIENDSHIP
& FAMILY

Calling all readers! Do you want to read a classic book that will tickle your mind? Well, you just can't miss with *Little Women* by Louisa May Alcott. "Sure," you say, "a classic?" Classics just may have been given a bad rap by people who don't read them.

Little Women is a story about four very different sisters. You will have a favorite of the four. You'll want her to win all of the arguments, get to travel, and find out the secrets. The March sisters have adventures, experience sadness and great times together. They are a cool family to get to know.

This is a book that you won't want to put down. It is a great book for traveling, because you'll be where you are going before you know it.

Every chapter keeps you wondering what will happen next. It's just like a television show that you can't wait to watch and don't want to end.

Put this on your "must read" list. You'll be glad you did.

Lauren Cooper, Grade 4
Swansboro, North Carolina

Author! Author!

Little Women is the story of Louisa May Alcott's own family. She modeled the character Jo after herself. The book made her rich. Her publisher had persuaded her to be paid in royalties (a small amount for each book sold) instead of a lump sum. Good decision—*Little Women* sold more than one million copies before Alcott's death in 1888.

The World's Best Jinx McGee

by Katherine Applegate

80 pages

CHALLENGE/
COURAGE

FRIENDSHIP
& FAMILY

HUMOR

The World's Best Jinx McGee is my favorite book. It's about a girl named Jinx McGee who used to be the best runner in the second grade—until the new girl came. Now Jinx is only second best, and that's not good enough. Everybody wants to be best at something. Jinx's friend Wanda is the best violin player, and Alex is the best reader. Maria can tell the best riddles. Even Jinx's dog is the best tail-wagger! Jinx wants to find something to be best at. But she never expected to be the wackiest, funniest, and best at making a fool of herself! I recommend this book to everybody who won't stop trying when at first they don't succeed. The illustrations are excellent.

Laura Martin, Grade 4
Woodrige, Illinois

Joe Montana

by Marc Appleman

128 pages

BIOGRAPHY

SPORTS

This exciting book tells about Joe Montana's life from when he was a kid playing football with his dad, being an all-sport champion in high school, winning a college championship to Notre Dame, to finally, making it to the pros where he won four Super Bowls for the 49ers.

This book makes me feel proud of Joe when he does great things, like winning the Super Bowl. It also made me feel sad when Joe had to struggle through seasons. I like Joe because he is a great player and is the best quarterback in history, but he is not so busy that he can't visit a boy who has a little more than two days to live.

I learned a lot about Joe's career by the stat box Marc Appleman put in the back of the book. It tells how many touchdowns Joe scored and how many yards he passed for each year.

If you like this book, you should read other biographies by Marc Appleman. They are: *Jim Abbott, Monica Seles,* and more!

Brian Goodman, Grade 4
Mohegan Lake, New York

Sounder

by William H. Armstrong

128 pages

ANIMAL

FRIENDSHIP & FAMILY

Do you like reading books about dogs and their loyalty to people? If you do, then *Sounder* is a great book for you. In the story, a poor black boy from the South tells how his father's coon dog, Sounder, risks his life to save his master. When his father, a sharecropper, is taken away to jail for stealing food to feed his family, Sounder tries to help him get free. Sounder is shot and disappears, badly hurt. The sad and lonely boy hopes that each new day will bring his father and dog back home. The story shows a lot of the good and bad in people, like courage, love, hate, and meanness. I like the book because it is a page-turner. I think when you read this story, you will like it, too.

Joseph DiRosario, Grade 5
Sumter, South Carolina

Author! Author!

William Armstrong grew up in Virginia. He loved to listen to stories told by an old man who was his friend. One night, when he was an adult, he heard a dog howling. The noise triggered a memory of one of those stories, about a dog named Sounder. Armstrong developed this memory into his award-winning book about loyalty.

Koala

by Caroline Arnold

48 pages

ANIMAL

If you are a nature lover, you will like *Koala*. Frangipani and her baby, Karen, live at Lone Pine Koala Sanctuary in southern Australia. A baby koala is only three-fourths of an inch long, or about the size of a lima bean, when it is born. A koala is four years old when it's full grown. When the baby koala is born, it has to climb up the mother's belly all by itself into the mother's pouch. If the koala falls off, it will die. Some of my favorite parts of the book were the great photographs of the koalas.

**Tyler Emrick, Grade 4
Parker, Colorado**

How Did We Find Out the Earth Is Round?

by Isaac Asimov

224 pages

ENVIRONMENT

HISTORY

Would you like a book that explains about people who lived long ago, who thought that Earth was flat, or that Earth went on forever? People thought that the sun rose in the west in the morning and traveled across the sky and set in the east in the evening. Some said there was a brand-new sun made every day.

The reason I liked this book was that it was interesting learning about the way people found out Earth was really round.

Author:
Isaac Asimov

**Kristina Marsella, Grade 3
Westchester, New York**

Norby and Yobo's Great Adventure

by Janet and Isaac Asimov

224 pages

HUMOR

SCIENCE FICTION

The main characters in *Norby and Yobo's Great Adventure* are two people named Jeff and Admiral Boris Yobo, and a robot named Norby. Admiral Yobo wants to go on a trip to find out the history of an heirloom. Norby "tunes into" the heirloom and uses his ability to travel back to prehistoric times. Then their adventures begin.

Norby and Yobo's Great Adventure is a science fiction book. I loved this book. It made me laugh. I recommend this book to anyone who dreams of having the ability to travel through time.

Tomas Echeverria, Grade 3
Albuquerque, New Mexico

Mr. Popper's Penguins

by Richard and Florence Atwater

148 pages

ANIMAL

FRIENDSHIP & FAMILY

HUMOR

Mr. Popper's Penguins is about a painter who lived with his wife, son, and daughter. He would stay up until midnight just reading about Antarctica. He loved penguins and accidentally ordered a penguin over the radio. He was so stunned when Drake Antarctic Expeditions' men came with the penguin. When his children came home from school, they saw it sitting in the refrigerator and thought they were dreaming. When Mrs. Popper came home from a meeting, she didn't like the idea that every time she opened the refrigerator there was a penguin there to hand her the food. Mr. Popper decided to name his penguin Captain Cook. The next thing Captain Cook did was hop into the bathtub for a nice cold bath. Then Captain Cook went to Broadway, and both Captain and Mr. Popper's family were famous and had tons of adventures. This book is very funny. Your whole family would probably like this book and many others by Richard and Florence Atwater.

Lacey Ann Hall, Grade 4
Emporia, Kansas

Teamwork

After Richard Atwater finished writing *Mr. Popper's Penguins,* he became very sick and never got better. His wife sent the story to several publishers, but everyone rejected it. So she rewrote parts of it to make it seem more believable. Then it was accepted! Almost 60 years later, it is still a favorite story.

Glass Slippers Give You Blisters

by Mary Jane Auch `176 pages`

CHALLENGE/ COURAGE

FRIENDSHIP & FAMILY

HUMOR

When Kelly tries out for a school play, she makes a total fool of herself. She sings badly in front of the cast while trying to imitate the older girl who sang beautifully. Embarrassed, she ends up joining the scenery crew. She is a fabulous artist. The only problem is that Kelly has to learn to speak up or her ideas will not be used.

I recommend this book to anyone looking for a humorous book to relate to. I'm sure almost everyone has made a fool of themselves at one time or another in front of a large group of people. This book made me feel better about some of the times I've said things in front of a large group that I wish I hadn't said. Kelly makes you realize everyone makes mistakes.

**Emily Vlasek, Grade 6
Bay Village, Ohio**

The True Confessions of Charlotte Doyle

by Avi `224 pages`

ADVENTURE

CHALLENGE/ COURAGE

HISTORY

This book is about a thirteen-year-old girl named Charlotte Doyle. She is going to her parents in Rhode Island. She has to travel with a rugged crew for two months. She is the only girl on the boat.

The book starts out in England on the docks of Liverpool in 1832. Charlotte is the kind of girl who stands up for what she believes in. But on the way to Rhode Island, she is tried and convicted of murder.

The character Charlotte Doyle reminds me of me. I stand up for what I believe in just like Charlotte did.

If you want to read about the adventures and hardships of a thirteen-year-old girl going to America in 1832, this book is for you.

**Michael Annabelle Comisar, Grade 5
Cincinnati, Ohio**

Harriet Tubman: The Road to Freedom

by Rae Bains

48 pages

BIOGRAPHY

CHALLENGE/ COURAGE

HISTORY

This biography is about a slave whose dream of freedom led her to become a conductor of the Underground Railroad. This brave slave was Harriet Tubman. The story tells about slavery and Tubman's role in fighting for her people's freedom.

I like this book because it gives interesting facts about the history of my people. It also has very nice photos. It was very interesting to see the people in the photographs, the way they looked, how they were dressed, and where they lived.

**Deshaunta Mchoy, Grade 6
Hallsboro, North Carolina**

Railroad Without Tracks

Harriet Tubman was a conductor on the Underground Railroad, a network of escape routes for runaway slaves. Kind people helped "passengers" heading to Canada and freedom. Sometimes they hid them from slave hunters. They also provided shelter, food, and medical care.

I, Houdini: The Autobiography of a Self-Educated Hamster

by Lynne Reid Banks

128 pages

ANIMAL

HUMOR

This is the story of an escape-artist hamster named Houdini. No cage could hold him. I really liked the book because I like to read adventure stories. I felt excited when I read about how Houdini could squeeze himself through the skinny bars of his cage. Another time he moved all of his stuff over to one side of his cage so it would tip over and he could get out. This made the owners very upset, because they could never be sure where to find him. They even tried to put him in a tall wastepaper basket, but nothing worked.

The best part of the book was when he met a field mouse. They became best friends and . . . oops, you'll have to read the book to find out what happens to them. This book reminds me of Beverly Cleary's books, *Runaway Ralph* and *Ralph and His Motorcycle,* because neither the mouse nor the hamster could be held in a cage too long.

**Lauran Ortman, Grade 5
Buffalo, New York**

Who-Dini?

Houdini Hamster was named after the legendary escape artist Harry Houdini. Harry Houdini amazed crowds by escaping from handcuffs, straitjackets, and many famous prisons. He once escaped from chains and ropes while locked in a trunk that was dropped into the New York harbor—in 59 seconds!

The Indian in the Cupboard

by Lynne Reid Banks

192 pages

ADVENTURE

FANTASY & FOLKLORE

FRIENDSHIP & FAMILY

The Indian in the Cupboard is about a kid named Omri. On his birthday, he gets a cupboard—not just any cupboard, but a magical cupboard where you can lock a plastic toy in it, and the toy becomes real. Well, Omri sticks an Indian in the cupboard, and he becomes real. Omri does not know what to do with him. So he keeps him for a while. They go through lots of adventures together.

In the middle of the story, Omri makes a cowboy come to life. The cowboy and Indian start to fight because cowboys and Indians usually don't mix. Then one day the cowboy, Boone, gets out of hand, and the Indian shoots him with an arrow.

If you like cowboys and Indians, I recommend this book. It has a lot of adventure. I won't tell you the ending—read it yourself.

Alexander Monterrubio, Grade 4
Fremont, California

The Mystery of the Cupboard

by Lynne Reid Banks

256 pages

ADVENTURE

FANTASY & FOLKLORE

FRIENDSHIP & FAMILY

This book is about a boy named Omri. Omri's parents decided to move to the country after a freak storm in London. Omri's mother inherited the house from her mother, Lottie. One night, Omri gets out of bed and trips on a book and a cashbox. The book is a diary of his great aunt, Jessica Charlotte Driscoll. Jessica had a son named Frederick who made tin toys. Frederick was thrown out of business by plastic toys, so he grew to hate them. He made a cupboard and put his hate for plastic into it. Now, when somebody puts a plastic figure in the cupboard, something very special happens.

I just gave you a hint to the secret of the cupboard that Omri finds out by reading the whole diary. I guess I should let you read the book before I spoil it for you. My opinion of this book is that it was wonderful! It is so intriguing that I did not want to put it down! It is a great mixture of mystery and fantasy. I know I'll cherish this book forever.

Sun-Hee Goldsberry, Grade 5
Sumter, South Carolina

Return of the Indian

by Lynne Reid Banks

ADVENTURE

FANTASY & FOLKLORE

FRIENDSHIP & FAMILY

Omri and Patrick are at it again: They are turning plastic soldiers into real people to help Little Bear's tribe. Omri finds out he can go back to Little Bear's time too! This book makes me feel happy because there is always some exciting event. I liked the main characters. They are always funny and cool! I wouldn't change any of the book. It is perfect and complete. This book makes me think of how much fun it would be to travel back in time!

Zack Ahmed, Grade 5
Alta Loma, California

Fan Power!

Lynne Reid Banks wrote the sequel to *The Indian in the Cupboard* after receiving many requests from children around the world. She included ideas the kids sent to her. Other authors have responded to kids, too. Roald Dahl made changes to *Charlie and the Chocolate Factory* after children objected to descriptions of some of the characters.

The Secret of the Indian

by Lynne Reid Banks

ADVENTURE

FANTASY & FOLKLORE

FRIENDSHIP & FAMILY

I loved reading *The Secret of the Indian*.

The main characters are Omri, Patrick, Emma, Little Bear, and Boone. Omri and Patrick are best friends. Emma is Patrick's cousin. Little Bear and Boone are dolls who are brought to life by a magical key. This story takes place in Omri's house in London.

Patrick has gone back in time. While Patrick is back in time, Omri is forced to tell the secret of the key to Emma. When Patrick comes back, he brings a disastrous cyclone from the past.

I am like Omri in the story, because I like to play with action figures. I enjoyed reading this book because the toys come to life.

Nikko Cavestany, Grade 4
Bedford, Connecticut

Author:
Lynne Reid
Banks

Cloudy With a Chance of Meatballs

by Judi Barrett

Cloudy With a Chance of Meatballs is a strange book. Who would think food could fall out of the sky? If pizza, ice cream, soup, peas, corn, and hamburgers fell out of the sky, would it be so great? Read the book and find out.

**Andrea Zirbel, Grade 3
Florence, South Dakota**

Turn Homeward, Hannalee

by Patricia Beatty

Guns firing, cannons blazing, innocent civilians being killed by the thousands! Being around during the Civil War was horrifying.

Twelve-year-old Hannalee Reed and her brother are taken from their home in Georgia to work in the North. This story is about Hannalee's dangerous, yet exciting, journey home.

Many of the events in this book are true, but exactly how or when they happened is probably unknown. Unlike many books about war, this one is light-hearted and not heavy or dense. I liked it because it is a real adventure! Two children, all alone, travel across the United States in the middle of the Civil War!

**Sarah Lustbader, Grade 5
New York, New York**

Author! Author!

Patricia Beatty wrote a number of books about the Civil War. These books incorporate many details from her mother's stories about the hardships of living in Kansas in the 1860s. Beatty also wrote 11 novels with her author-husband, John Beatty.

Who Comes with Cannons?

by Patricia Beatty

192 pages

ADVENTURE

FRIENDSHIP & FAMILY

HISTORY

Who Comes with Cannons is about a Quaker girl named Truth, during the Civil War. Truth was sent to South Carolina from Indiana to live with her aunt and uncle, because her mother died and her father was dying in a hospital.

When I heard about the book I wanted to read it because I especially enjoy historical fiction. Truth's new family was involved in helping runaway slaves. One part of the book that really caught my interest was when Truth's cousins were forced to fight in the Civil War, but being Quakers neither of them wanted to fight. One cousin was taken to prison by the northerners. Then Truth went on a wonderful adventure to rescue her cousin from the prison.

From *Who Comes with Cannons?* I learned what Quaker life was like, and what they had to deal with during the Civil War.

Guiliva Avanzato, Grade 5
Oneonta, New York

Emily

by Michael Bedard

40 pages

BIOGRAPHY

DRAMA

FRIENDSHIP & FAMILY

If you like good biographies, then I have a book for you. *Emily* is about a woman who stayed in her house with only music and poetry as her window to the outside world.

In this story, nobody knew her name except one little girl. One day, Emily wanted that little girl to play music for her. She did, and that was the only time anybody ever saw Emily.

This is a true story about a real lady named Emily Dickinson. I thought it was a great book, and the artwork was really the center of attention. I thought it was like no other book I have ever read!

Ana Muniz, Grade 4
Tucson, Arizona

A Real Character

Emily Dickinson was a real person. As an adult, she always dressed in white and almost never left her house and garden in Amherst, Massachusetts. Many people once thought her unrhymed poetry was as strange as her lifestyle. Modern readers usually hail her poems as the work of a creative genius.

The Eyes of the Killer Robot

by John Bellairs

160 pages

MYSTERY

SCIENCE FICTION

The Eyes of the Killer Robot is an exciting mystery. You always want to know what's going to happen next. The story is about a kid named Johnny, a professor named Professor Childermass, a teenager named Fergie, and a mad scientist named Evaristus Sloane. The mad scientist is trying to take Johnny's eyes to use for his new robot. He's making a robot to rob things. Meanwhile, Professor Childermass and Fergie are trying to find Johnny to save him. My favorite part is when Fergie and Johnny find the first clue. The clue is a glass eye in a box that was in a broken-down baseball stadium. Even if you don't love mysteries, you'll love this book.

STAR REVIEW

Zane Carney, Grade 3
Actor

Gwinna

by Barbara Helen Berger

128 pages

FANTASY & FOLKLORE

This book is about a woodworker and his wife. They longed for a child for many years. Finally, the woman said that they should go to the mother of the owls. Many people said that the mother of the owls was very evil, but others said that she was very wise. They decided to go to the mother of the owls, despite the risks. Soon the woman and her husband walked toward the forest with nobody seeing them (the mother of owls lived in the forest).

When they got to the forest, they made a bargain. The mother of the owls said that if she gave the woodworker and his wife a child, they would have to give her back the child when the child turned twelve.

Is the child returned to the mother of the owls? Read this amazing tale and find out.

Deanna Talens, Grade 4
Appleton, Wisconsin

Kate's Turn

by Jeanne Betancourt

192 pages

This book is about a young girl named Kate who goes to the American Ballet school in New York City. Other girls from other states and countries live in one house with a lady who takes care of them. Kate goes to school between dance classes. She learns how hard it is to become a dancer. Some of the girls get hurt or sick and have to stop dancing and go home. Will this happen to her, too?

This book reminds me of myself, because I love to dance. I learned about some of the things that can happen from dancing and that not everyone gets to the top. This book made me think about what I want to do with my life when I grow up. I do want to be a dancer, but I could always be a dance teacher.

Shaina Rhodes, Grade 6
Port Jefferson, New York

The Heroine of the Titanic: A Tale Both True and Otherwise of the Life of Molly Brown

by Joan W. Blos

40 pages

I read a fantastic book called *The Heroine of the Titanic*. I liked this book and I think you'll like it too. It made me feel talented and brave just like her. This book reminds me of my mother, because she is a widow and she is very brave. The artwork in the book helps you follow the story like you were really there.

I recommend this book to anybody who likes adventure. You definitely will be going on an adventure with Molly Brown at sea. Just think, kids, you or I may be a hero or a heroine some day!

Maryann Scorzello, Grade 4
Mahopac, New York

A Titanic Disaster

In 1912, the "unsinkable" *Titanic* was the largest ocean liner in the world—as long as four city blocks. But on its first trip, it struck an iceberg and sank. Of the 2,200 people on board, only about 700 survived, most of them women and children. The *Titanic* was one of the first ships to use the signal SOS (Save Our Ship).

Are You There, God? It's Me, Margaret

by Judy Blume

156 pages

CHALLENGE/ COURAGE

FRIENDSHIP & FAMILY

HUMOR

Author: Judy Blume

This wonderful story was written from a young girl's point of view. I think Judy Blume thought back to her childhood in order to get Margaret's, the main character's, feelings straight.

I liked Margaret. She thought over her many problems with God. She moved to a new town where she didn't know anyone. She thought she didn't fit in with her new friends. She was almost twelve years old and didn't go to church. Her new friends either went to the Y or the Jewish Community Center. Margaret wasn't practicing a religion. Her mother was Catholic and her father was Jewish. To keep her grandparents from fighting, her parents had decided not to practice either religion.

Margaret reminded me of one of my friends. She and Margaret are alike in many ways. They both worry about the changes that take place as they get older. This book left me a lot to think about. One thing was, what it would feel like to not be any religion.

I think this book is for preteen girls. Other people just wouldn't understand how Margaret felt. To find out more about Margaret's way of thinking and how she hides her feelings from others, read *Are You There, God? It's Me, Margaret* by the magnificent author, Judy Blume.

> **Rachel Kudrich, Grade 6**
> **Matamoras, Pennsylvania**

Freckle Juice

by Judy Blume

48 pages

HUMOR

Freckle Juice is an entertaining story. Andrew wanted to have freckles so he wouldn't have to wash his neck and behind his ears. He thought freckles would keep his mom from seeing his dirty neck. Andrew's classmate, Sharon, knew how much he wanted freckles. She sold him her recipe even though she knew it wouldn't work. Andrew finally came up with his own idea for making freckles.

I liked this book because Andrew learned that it is better to think for yourself than to listen to other people.

> **J. Trevor Colburn, Grade 7**
> **Takoma Park, Maryland**

Fudge-a-Mania

by Judy Blume

FRIENDSHIP & FAMILY

HUMOR

Fudge-a-Mania is a very interesting book. There are two boys and a baby girl. The oldest boy's name is Peter; he usually gets blamed for the things his little brother does. The little boy's name is Fudge; he wants to be a bird when he grows up. The baby's name is Tootsie. Then there is Sheila Tubman, who ends up being Fudge's baby-sitter. Fudge wants to marry Sheila so no monsters will eat him up. Then Fudge meets a girl who ends up being his friend, and she has a secret formula for monster spray. I like it when they swirl around singing and laughing because they have Fudge-a-Mania. This book makes me feel I am right there in the story. It reminds me of my brother and sister, who like to get each other into trouble. I would recommend this book to others because it's enjoyable, funny, and mischievous. It is such a good book I read it twenty times, and I think you might do the same thing.

**Theresa Stoeckell, Grade 6
Binghamton, New York**

Here's to You, Rachel Robinson

by Judy Blume

CHALLENGE/ COURAGE

FRIENDSHIP & FAMILY

Here's to You, Rachel Robinson is about a seventh grade girl named Rachel Robinson. Rachel is a terrific student; she gets straight A's and probably could be nicknamed Miss Perfect!

Rachel has two best friends named Stephanie and Alison. Rachel is a normal kid, just real tall and smart. She feels her life is fine and happy, until her brother Charles gets kicked out of boarding school.

Charles went to boarding school because he didn't get along with the family. To Rachel it seems like Charles lives to be cruel!

When Charles first comes home, Rachel thinks her life is falling apart, but then she kisses this cute boy named Jeremy that she and her friends have always gone gaga over. Maybe Rachel's life isn't so bad, after all!

This book is definitely a book you've got to read! If you don't, you're really missing out on one fabulous book!!!

**Bethany Toellner, Grade 5
Sedalia, Missouri**

It's Not the End of the World

by Judy Blume

176 pages

CHALLENGE/
COURAGE

FRIENDSHIP
& FAMILY

One of my favorite books is *It's Not the End of the World*. Karen's parents are going to get divorced. Karen's not getting along with friends or family because of it. Her dad introduces her to a girl who's older and has gone through it all before. Because of the divorce, many problems arise. For example, her mom and brother get in a fight and her brother runs away. How is Karen going to get her parents back together before her parents make it final? You can find out if you read Judy Blume's book, *It's Not the End of the World*.

Author:
Judy Blume

**Ariane Eicke, Grade 5
Riverton, Wyoming**

Just as Long as We're Together

by Judy Blume

304 pages

CHALLENGE/
COURAGE

FRIENDSHIP
& FAMILY

This book is about Rachel and Stephanie, who have been best friends since second grade. They have shared all their secrets, good and bad; so when Alison moves to town, Stephanie hopes they can all be best friends. I like this book because it tells about the changes in their lives and how they deal with them. I think everyone should read this book because it is funny and exciting.

**Kristen Kaminskas, Grade 5
Hamden, Connecticut**

Mail Call

Judy Blume receives about 2,000 letters a month from readers! To write to her or other writers and illustrators, follow these tips:

1. Send your letter care of the book's publisher. The address will be on the copyright page. Or look up the address in *The Kid's Address Book* by Michael Levine.

2. Keep your letter short. Print clearly or type.

3. Send a self-addressed, stamped envelope for a reply.

Starring Sally J. Freedman as Herself

by Judy Blume

`240 pages`

ADVENTURE

CHALLENGE/ COURAGE

FRIENDSHIP & FAMILY

HISTORY

One of my favorite books is called *Starring Sally J. Freedman as Herself*. The story is about a ten year old Jewish girl named Sally who moves to Florida because of her big brother's bad health. It takes place a little after World War II. I learned about having to make new friends, living in a different home, and adjusting to a new school. I enjoyed reading about Sally's fun personality and how her thoughts and dreams were creative and funny. This book reminded me of the "Molly" books in the American Girls series in many ways. *Starring Sally J. Freedman as Herself* is a delightful book, and I recommend it to any girl who likes to read about friendship, hard times, and adventure.

Alicia Perry, Grade 5
Flower Mound, Texas

Author! Author!

Do you like books that are warm and funny? Do you like to read about kids who have real problems, like confronting racism, going through puberty, or having parents divorce? Then read some of Judy Blume's books. You might especially enjoy *Starring Sally J. Freedman as Herself*, which contains many incidents and details from Blume's own childhood.

Superfudge

by Judy Blume

`176 pages`

FRIENDSHIP & FAMILY

HUMOR

Superfudge is one of my favorite books because it is so funny. It's about a kid named Peter who can't live with his brother, Fudge, because he is very, very, annoying. Then Peter finds out there is a new member coming to the family pretty soon. Now Peter is not only mad, he is worried. What if the baby turns out like Fudge? Then he finds out he's moving to New Jersey. Peter just doesn't like all of these changes. He misses the sounds of the city, and when the baby is born, he actually misses getting sleep at night. Peter also misses having normal parents. After naming a kid Fudge, they named the new baby Tootsie! Talk about abnormal. Hey! You don't think I'm actually going to spoil the book for you, do you? I guess you'll just have to read the book for yourself.

P.S. After reading *Superfudge,* try the two sequels: *Fudge-a-Mania,* and *Tales of a Fourth Grade Nothing.*

Carrie Holtgrefe, Grade 4
Cincinnati, Ohio

Tales of a Fourth Grade Nothing

by Judy Blume

128 pages

Tales of a Fourth Grade Nothing is a great book, especially for kids who have annoying little brothers or sisters. The book is about a nine-year-old boy named Peter who has a bothersome little brother named Fudge. Fudge is always doing stupid things, like scribbling on Peter's homework or spreading mashed potatoes on the walls of Hamburger Heaven. One of my favorite parts is when Fudge's friend Jenny is over to play, and she wets her pants on purpose! I know it doesn't sound very funny the way I put it, but the way the book puts it, it was hilarious! I liked this book because it is well written, detailed, and funny. It also gives you enough information to really know what is going on in the story.

Jackie Geewax, Grade 3
West Grove, Pennsylvania

Tales of a Fourth Grade Nothing

by Judy Blume

128 pages

Have you ever read a book with little stories about one person? Well, if you have read *Tales of a Fourth Grade Nothing*, then you have. This is one funny book. It is about two brothers, Peter and Fudge. Fudge is two years old and gets into lots of trouble. Peter is ten years old and tries to stop Fudge from getting into trouble.

The book made me feel excited because I never knew what was going to happen next. For example, Fudge was playing on the jungle gym. He wanted to fly, so he pretended to be a bird and jumped off the jungle gym. But he fell on his face and swallowed his two front teeth!

This book has lots of pictures, but not any color. I did not feel the pictures needed color because the book made you form pictures in your mind. Judy Blume described everything so well.

This book is funny because Peter would tell his mother that Fudge should not do all the things he did because he was too young. But his mother would always say, "Nonsense!" As it always turned out, Peter was right. I definitely recommend this to other kids.

Liz Pretzinger, Grade 5
Cincinnati, Ohio

Tiger Eyes

by Judy Blume

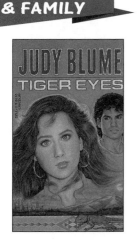

224 pages

"Some changes happen deep down inside of you. And the truth is only what you know about them. Maybe that's the way it's supposed to be." That is a quote from *Tiger Eyes*. It is my favorite part.

Tiger Eyes is a very emotional book. A girl named Davey, who is in her teens, has to go through a lot of pain. Her dad died when he got shot while working in a drugstore. She has to adjust to a change of scene. Her mom has become invisible, and she has to listen to her aunt and uncle who are overprotective. She meets two new friends who disappear out of her life. Then she has to face moving back to the place where her father was killed. I learned that life isn't as people think it is. People suffer all over the world, and we don't even care about it.

If you like books that have a lot of emotion and feelings, I prescribe *Tiger Eyes* for you. Remember, believe in yourself, not what others think about you. That's what I think *Tiger Eyes* is about.

Ashley Caravella, Grade 6
Somers, Connecticut

Sinbad the Sailor

by Bonny Books

32 pages

If you like adventure stories, boy do I have a book for you. The book is *Sinbad the Sailor*. It is a book about a boy named Sinbad who is very rich and lives in a palace. His dream is not to live in the palace all of his life, but to sail the seven seas. Sinbad's wish was granted, and he sails off on his wild and scary adventures.

I learned from this book that if you ever have a chance to go on an adventure, you should go, because you might not ever get the chance again.

This is a very interesting book and I liked it a lot. The artwork is colorful and neat, and it gave me an idea of what the characters looked like and what they were doing. If you like adventure stories like I do, then you should read this book!!!

Sam Vanini, Grade 3
Lancaster, New York

Mozart: Scenes from the Childhood of the Great Composer

by Catherine Brighton

32 pages

Mozart is an amazing book about a real person. The main characters are Joannes Chrysostomus Wolfgangus Amadeus Mozart and his sister, Maria Anna Walburga Ignatia Mozart. They lived in Salzburg, Austria. Their father wrote music for Count Schrattenbach. He taught Wolfi and Nannerl, as they were called by their parents, music and to play many instruments. By the time he was nine years old, Mozart played for kings and queens around the world. He was treated like royalty. He was so famous that the artist Lorenzoni was chosen to paint his portrait. He became friends with another great composer, Johann Bach. Many people thought he was a fraud, but he proved them wrong. He almost died of smallpox. By the time he was eleven years old, he was a world-famous composer. This book has many beautiful pictures and is very good. If you would like to read this book, you can find it at the library or bookstore.

Amanda Russo, Grade 4
Medford, Massachusetts

Genius!

Mozart, born in 1756, was a musical genius. He composed his first piece at five, his first symphony at eight, and his first opera at twelve. Altogether, he composed more than 600 pieces—and he died at the age of 36! He said that his compositions often just flowed out of his head, perfect the first time.

Your Best Friend, Kate

by Pat Brisson

40 pages

Kate and her family go on a trip by car through eleven states and Washington, D.C. Kate writes to her friend Lucy from each state and tells her about interesting places they visit. The pictures show what they saw, what the state flower is, what the state tree is, and the state bird. I found out that the cardinal is the state bird of North Carolina, Kentucky, and Ohio. Kate and her brother, Brian, don't get along well. Brian and Kate remind me of my sister, Michelle, and me.

I thought the book was excellent.

Matt Pryor, Grade 4
Arkport, New York

Medical Mysteries: Six Deadly Cases

by Dian Dincin Buchman

112 pages

MYSTERY

Medical Mysteries is about six deadly medical mysteries that are true and what people do to solve them. One of the cases is "The Moving Freckle"—a tick that infects people. Doctors have to find out what is causing the disease to spread. Another case is "The Mystery of the Poisoned Boys." It is about a few boys who buy some blue jeans and are poisoned. "The Hidden Time Bomb" is about a town where one by one the people get sick and don't know why. One of my favorites was "The Hunt for Baffling Bacteria." It is about many people catching Legionnaires' disease. A scientist discovered something that no professional could see. "Unraveling a Riddle" is about pellagra, a very bad disease that could kill you. Three little boys living in an orphanage gave the doctor the last clue to the 200-year-old case.

Is There a Detective in the House?

Epidemiologists (eh-pe-dee-me-AH-la-jists) are the medical experts who try to figure out sources of baffling diseases. They also track the frequency and spread of ordinary illnesses, like the flu. They have to be part doctor, part detective. They use everything from common sense to elaborate computer technology to make their diagnoses.

I think Dian Buchman wrote this book to teach kids about many mysterious diseases that can kill you and how doctors figured out what caused them. She made the stories interesting to read by writing them like mysteries.

**Katie Shetler, Grade 5
St. Augustine, Florida**

The Jolly Man

by Jimmy Buffet and Savannah Jane Buffett

32 pages

ADVENTURE

FANTASY & FOLKLORE

MULTICULTURAL

Do you like books about magical adventures? Well, then, you will like *The Jolly Man,* by singer/songwriter Jimmy Buffet and his daughter, Savannah Jane Buffet. It is about a fisherman from Bananaland. He has a magic voice that can sing fish out of the sea. One day, he finds a magic guitar that leads to many adventures in the Caribbean Sea with different groups of island people, a gang of pirates headed by one-eyed Rosy, and a very special dolphin. I like this book because it is also a song, and the beautiful illustrations bring the song to life.

**Alex Yucas, Grade 3
Pittsburgh, Pennsylvania**

Hut School and the Wartime Home Front Heroes

by Robert Burch

144 pages

I loved *Hut School and the Wartime Home Front Heroes*. It's about a group of sixth-grade students who live in Redhill, Georgia, at the time of World War II. Due to overpopulation, the class must have school in a hut, which is why they call it "Hut School." I love the book because it's full of drama and suspense, and it's hysterically funny. The book made me feel like I was right there at the time of the war. It's so easy to get into it. The book has simple pencil artwork. The illustrator, Robert Himler, picked the right things to illustrate, but illustrations were not needed. I would recommend this book to anyone in fourth grade and up who is interested in what it was like to live at the time of the war.

Jonathan Tarella, Grade 4
East Brunswick, New Jersey

Ida Early Comes Over the Mountain

by Robert Burch

152 pages

Ida Early Comes Over the Mountain is one great book! The main character is Ida Early. I like Ida because she is happy and cheerful, like me. Ida is always busy either solving a problem or playing with the four kids she minds: Ellen, Randall, and the twins, Clay and Dewey. The book takes place near the Blue Ridge Mountains in Georgia.

The story begins when Ida Early comes over the mountain to the Suttons' house. Ida moves in and begins to take care of the family. When Ida takes Clay and Dewey to school, she is teased by some older kids, which makes her feel sad. After several days, Ida leaves. Ellen and Randall realize that they should have stopped their friends' meanness. The family misses Ida and has to get along without her. One day, she comes back, and the family is happy again.

I think this is a good book because it leaves you happy. I learned that you should try to come to the defense of a friend.

Ellen Gaintner, Grade 4
El Cerrito, California

The Secret Garden

by Frances Hodgson Burnett

288 pages

This book is about a girl named Mary Lennox whose parents die. She has to move to a big house in the country with her uncle. She is a very bossy, lonely, disagreeable girl. When she finds the "Secret Garden," she's a totally different person. She makes friends and lives happily.

This book makes me feel like I'm in it, because you could do anything that the people in the book do. My sister acts like Mary Lennox when she is in a bad mood. I learned that I'm very friendly compared to Mary. This book is very interesting, and I think if you like to read you will enjoy it.

**Morgan Kremers, Grade 5
Ft. Smith, Arkansas**

Classic! Classic!

How do you create a classic? Frances Hodgson Burnett knew the key: believable characters. Her characters have flaws, like Mary's sour temper, that make them seem real. To create her enduring characters and stories, Burnett drew on her own childhood experiences. She used to play in a "secret" garden near her home.

The Incredible Journey

by Sheila Burnford

160 pages

The Incredible Journey is about two dogs and a cat that run away and travel over 100 miles to get to where their owner lives. To survive such a task they must hunt, stay together, escape danger, and help each other.

One big problem they have was when the cat got into a fight with a lynx. Another problem is when all three of them have to fight off two bears. The third problem I will tell you about is when the Labrador is hunting. He sees a porcupine and tries to fight it, and gets quills all over his cheek and neck. One quill even works its way into his mouth.

Will they survive all these disasters? Can they get back to their master's house? If you want to find out what happens, you have to read the book yourself.

**Timothy LaPointe, Grade 5
Port Jefferson, New York**

The Summer of the Swans

by Betsy Byars

144 pages

CHALLENGE/
COURAGE

FRIENDSHIP
& FAMILY

I thought *The Summer of the Swans* was a boring book in the beginning, until an enormous reversal took place. The excitement started when Charlie, a main character, disappeared. Everyone was so worried, especially his sister, Sara. Charlie had a bad fever when he was three, which caused brain damage.

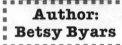

Author:
Betsy Byars

   I could feel being as frightened as Charlie felt after he wandered off and became lost in the woods. While Sara searched for him, I could feel how worried she was and how much she loved Charlie. I felt as if I was there in the search. I look forward to reading this author's next book.

**Gregory Heeber, Grade 5
Copiague, New York**

Wanted... Mud Blossom

by Betsy Byars

160 pages

ADVENTURE

HUMOR

MYSTERY

If you like books with excitement and adventure, then *Wanted . . . Mud Blossom* is the book for you. Tragedy strikes at the Blossoms' house. First, Mad Mary, a family friend, is missing. Then Mud, the family dog, is accused of eating Junior Blossom's class hamster. The only way they can solve the case is by putting Mud on trial! This is a great book and I highly recommend it to everyone!

**Alexis Rupp, Grade 5
Bryan, Ohio**

Author! Author!

Some authors outline every detail before they begin. Others write the endings first. Betsy Byars has an unusual approach. First, she thinks of a title. Then she types it up, sits back and thinks, "I just need four thousand sentences to go with this, and I'll have a book."

Julian, Secret Agent

by Ann Cameron

FRIENDSHIP & FAMILY

HUMOR

MYSTERY

If you read this book, you will love it! The author, Ann Cameron, wrote this book with good describing words. That means she paints great pictures in our minds. I think she really understands kids. Just so you'll get interested in the story, I'll tell you part of it. Well, Julian and Gloria and Huey are at the post office when they find a picture of a criminal, and they think they can find him. So they call themselves the "Crime Busters." First, they find a dog stuck in a hot car, then they rescue a toddler from drowning, then . . . well, you'll have to read the rest of the book to find out. This book is called *Julian, Secret Agent* if you want to check it out at the library. It is so good you can never put it down when you are reading it. Well, I hope you enjoy this book. I bet 100% of you will.

**Krista Vargas, Grade 4
Avon, Indiana**

The Family Under the Bridge

by Natalie Savage Carlson

CHALLENGE/ COURAGE

DRAMA

FRIENDSHIP & FAMILY

The Family Under the Bridge is one of the most charming Christmas stories I've ever read! It is about this hobo named Armand who lives in Paris. Every winter, Armand returns to a certain bridge by the Seine River for shelter. But one winter, things change. Armand finds a family already settled in his spot under the bridge. At first, Armand is angry. But after a while, he grows attached to the children and their mother. I think this is a great book and I definitely recommend it—especially at Christmastime!

Chelsea Crucy, Grade 4 ·········
Mohegan Lake, New York

Elaine and the Flying Frog

by Heidi Chang

This book is about a girl named Elaine Chow who moves from San Francisco to Iowa and is very unhappy. One day at lunch a girl at Elaine's table sees her eating fried rice and makes fun of her because she thinks Elaine is different. Then Elaine meets a girl named Mary Lewis at her school and they become good friends. One day, their teacher assigns a class project—to bring in a flying object. Wait until you see what Elaine and Mary Lewis decide to bring!

I thought this was a very good book because I know it's hard to make changes and to go to places you've never been before. If you are like me and have moved, you will like this book.

**Whitney Lester, Grade 3
Longmont, Colorado**

A Separate Battle: Women and the Civil War

by Ina Chang

My favorite book is called *A Separate Battle: Women and the Civil War*. I like this book because it doesn't just tell you what men had to do in the Civil War. It also tells you about the part women played in the war. The jobs women held included being a spy, a farmer, and a nurse. Some of the women in this book are Harriet Beecher Stowe, Harriet Tubman, and Clara Barton.

One important thing women did was hold a large fair to raise money for the people in the war. The fair was a huge success. They raised more than two million dollars.

**Samantha Bathija, Grade 6
Stamford, Connecticut**

History, Herstory

Books like *A Separate Battle* show us how women have shaped world events. To find out about influential women at other times and places, check out *The Book of Distinguished American Women* by Vincent Wilson, Jr., and *Herstory: Women Who Changed the World* by Ruth Ashby and Deborah Gore Ohrn.

What the Witch Left

by Ruth Chew

128 pages

ADVENTURE

FANTASY & FOLKLORE

THRILLS & CHILLS

What the Witch Left is an excellent book for someone who loves magic and adventure. Katy's aunt left some weird belongings in a dresser drawer. When Katy and her friend Louise unlock the drawer, they find a magical adventure ahead of them. Then they find out that the magic causes trouble—especially now that they have lost the key to the drawer. Her aunt is coming back and, if she is a witch, she won't be very happy!

Elizabeth Spille, Grade 5
Greenville, Ohio

Hard Drive to Short

by Matt Christopher

160 pages

CHALLENGE/ COURAGE

FRIENDSHIP & FAMILY

SPORTS

Hard Drive to Short is the greatest book! If you have a secret and you don't know if you should tell it or not, the answer will be in this fantastic book. It tells you how friends could become enemies, or stick together as pals.

Sandy Varga has a big secret. Whenever Sandy has a baseball game, she always has to leave early. Sandy's friends are getting real angry, because Sandy won't tell why he has to leave early. Sandy is afraid to tell them, because he thinks if he does, his friends will laugh at him. But if Sandy doesn't tell, will his friendships be lost forever?

If you want to know if Sandy will have enemies or friends, you'll just have to read this awesome book to find out.

Robert Lee, Grade 5
Addison, Illinois

Author! Author!

Matt Christopher is one of the most popular American sports writers for children, having written lots and lots of novels for kids. If you're one of his faithful readers, you might want to join his official fan club. You can send a self-addressed, stamped envelope along with $1 to:

Matt Christopher Fan Club
c/o Little, Brown and Company
34 Beacon Street
Boston, MA 02018

The Kid Who Only Hit Homers

by Matt Christopher

ADVENTURE

CHALLENGE/ COURAGE

SPORTS

160 pages

If you like realistic fiction books, you'll like *The Kid Who Only Hit Homers.* This book reminds me of *Return of the Home Run Kid* because they have the same characters and one of them is on a winning streak both times. This is a perfect third-grade book, but there are some difficult words. I think Matt Christopher is one of the best authors. I chose the book because I like his writing style. This book is about a kid named Sylvester who wants to be the best player in the town but really isn't very good, until he meets Mr. Barruth, and now he hits a home run every time. This book has two very important lessons in the game of life. You can do anything if you put your mind to it, and don't cheat. It's a lot more fun if you play fair.

Logan Beebe, Grade 3
Laguna Hills, California

The Kid Who Only Hit Homers

by Matt Christopher

ADVENTURE

CHALLENGE/ COURAGE

SPORTS

160 pages

In *The Kid Who Only Hit Homers,* a kid named Sylvester Coddmyer III wanted to quit baseball because he couldn't hit or judge the ball. I liked and disliked the main character because he quit baseball, but when he got some advice, all he could hit were homers. The artwork in this book is great because it really shows his expression. I would change the way the story is, and I would have different leagues. The things I learned are: never give up, and try your hardest. It reminded me of my father. He used to hit everything. The other book it reminds me of is *Too Hot to Handle* because it is also about baseball. The book helped me learn never to give up and don't be greedy. The book made me feel happy and sad, because Sylvester couldn't hit the ball but he never gave up.

Charles Ticker, Grade 5
Middlefield, Connecticut

You Make the Call!

Every book review is unique, because reviewers all have their own opinions, likes, and dislikes. Logan Beebe and Charles Ticker both liked *The Kid Who Only Hit Homers,* but for different reasons. As you read the book, think about the different reviews. Whose point of view is more like your own?

Miracle at the Plate

by Matt Christopher

CHALLENGE/ COURAGE

FRIENDSHIP & FAMILY

SPORTS

Miracle at the Plate is a good book about baseball. It's about a boy named Skeeter who hits very well but bats cross-handed. He plays left field.

Almost every time someone hits a fly ball to him, he stumbles on his long legs. A player on his team wants Skeeter not to start so his friend Tommy can start. Skeeter is also afraid to slide. Worst of all, Skeeter accidentally hit Tommy's dog.

You should read this book to find out what happens. It's very exciting. You should also read other Matt Christopher books.

Chip Darlington, Grade 5
Mentor, Ohio

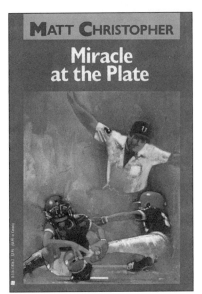

Doodle Soup

by John Ciardi

HUMOR

POETRY

Do you like wacky and silly poems? I do. That's why I suggest *Doodle Soup* by John Ciardi. This book made me feel silly. It reminds me of *Where the Sidewalk Ends,* because some of the poems in this book are almost like poems in *Where the Sidewalk Ends.* There isn't a whole lot of artwork in this book. I recommend it to people who are really into poetry. All I have to say is this book has a lot to do with people. It has a little to do with animals. And I think John Ciardi is a great poet.

Chrissy Dicker, Grade 5
Freemont, Ohio

A Writer's Corner

Inspired to write? Make yourself a studio. Include:

1. **Desk and chair.** A clipboard and cushion will do.
2. **Paper.** All sorts, lined and unlined.
3. **Writing instruments.** Pens, pencils, a computer or word processor, if possible.
4. **Office supplies.** Paper clips, stapler, tape, glue stick, stamps, envelopes.
5. **Bulletin board.** Tack up ideas, quotes, pictures, anything to jump-start your creativity!

Gross Facts to Blow Your Mind

by Judith Freeman Clark and Stephen Long `48 pages`

ANIMAL

ENVIRONMENT

HUMOR

Gross Facts to Blow Your Mind is a very cool book. Three of my favorite topics are "Hooked on You," "Open Wide," and "Don't Forget to Wash Behind Your Ears." It's not exactly a book that tells a story on one page and finishes it on the next. It's a book that tells four neat things on one page! "Don't Forget to Wash Behind Your Ears" is really neat. It's about bugs living on your eyelashes. I told my mom I didn't think it was real. I recommend this book to people who like neat things.

Chelsie Paige Cohen, Grade 3 ·············
Warminster, Pennsylvania

Beezus and Ramona

by Beverly Cleary `130 pages`

CHALLENGE/ COURAGE

HUMOR

Beezus and Ramona is about a girl named Beezus and her little sister, Ramona. Ramona is always making trouble, like when Beezus was in art class, her sister took a Blow Pop from a boy named Henry and caused lots of trouble.

I think the book is excellent because Ramona does lots of things wrong, and it reminds me of my sister, who can sometimes be a pain. I recommend this book to anyone who has little sister trouble.

Rachel Reckmeyer, Grade 4
Leesburg, Virginia

Author:
Beverly
Cleary

Author! Author!

Beverly Cleary was a Blackbird in first grade. The Blackbirds were the lowest reading group. She struggled with reading until third grade. Then one rainy day, she picked up a library book called *The Dutch Twins*. She loved it—and from then on she could read well and with pleasure.

The Mouse and the Motorcycle

by Beverly Cleary

ADVENTURE

ANIMAL

HUMOR

The Mouse and the Motorcycle is an exciting book. It is about a boy named Keith who develops a special friendship with a mouse named Ralph. I like Ralph because he is daring, especially with his little motorcycle. I am like Ralph because I like to take risks, too. Everyone should read this book because it will get your heart beating.

Walter Young, Grade 6
Seattle, Washington

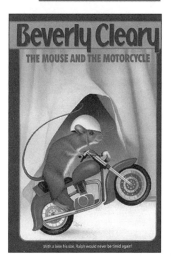

Muggie Maggie

by Beverly Cleary

CHALLENGE/
COURAGE

HUMOR

Maggie didn't want to learn cursive. She thought that writing cursive was very hard. It was a Monday morning and her teacher said that Maggie could be messenger for the week. She liked to be the messenger of the week. Maggie's teacher always wrote in cursive. That day, Maggie's teacher gave Maggie a note to give to the principal. On the way to the principal's office, Maggie wondered if her teacher wrote anything about her. She thought that a small peek wouldn't hurt. But it was written in cursive. She tried to read it, but she couldn't understand what it said. She went to the principal's office and gave her the note.

I like this book because it is about cursive. This year I am learning cursive in my class. I like writing cursive a lot! This book made me feel great because I like reading books about kids my age learning cursive.

This book reminded me of the troubles I had, like Maggie, when I was learning cursive. I also had to take a note to the principal once. But, of course, I didn't read it!

The artwork is excellent because it is in black and white. I think that the pictures look pretty in black and white.

I recommend this book to others because I enjoyed reading this book. I think you will, too! BYE!

Kirti Mahajan, Grade 3
Norristown, Pennsylvania

Ramona and Her Father

by Beverly Cleary

192 pages

CHALLENGE/ COURAGE

FRIENDSHIP & FAMILY

HUMOR

Everyone in Ramona's family was in a bad mood because her dad lost his job. Everything that Ramona was trying to do to cheer up her family was causing more trouble. Everyone was upset with her, even in school. Ramona knew that everything would be okay when her father told her he wouldn't trade her in for a million dollars. I liked this book because it has a happy ending. I recommend this book to kids my age because it is funny. The artwork is neat because it is sketches. The book has a great ending, but I won't spoil it for you.

**Michelle Daidone, Grade 4
Manteo, North Carolina**

Clomp! Clomp!

Like Ramona and Howie, Beverly Cleary loved clomping around on tin can stilts. You can, too! Here's how:

1. Take two empty one-pound coffee cans. Have an adult poke holes in either side with a nail.
2. Cut two lengths of heavy twine to extend from one hole, up to hip height, and back to the opposite hole. Thread through holes. Knot securely.
3. Stand on the cans, hold the strings, and start clomping!

Ramona and Her Mother

by Beverly Cleary

208 pages

CHALLENGE/ COURAGE

FRIENDSHIP & FAMILY

HUMOR

I loved *Ramona and Her Mother*. The story is about a seven-year-old girl named Ramona Quimby. The plot is about how Ramona thinks that Beezus, her older sister, is liked better than she is. In this story there are good things, bad things, and funny things that happen in this stage of her life.

On a scale of 1–10, I give this book a 9 because Beverly Cleary really makes you feel like you are seven years old. My favorite part in the book is when Ramona and her friend Howie make a wooden boat. They want to see if it could float, and when it does they decide to use a substance called bluing, which is a kind of bleach, to make the water look like the sea. When Ramona climbs up the shelf to get it, it pours all over them because the cap is loose. I thought that was a pretty funny part in the book. Now, how about you read it yourself!

**Alex Vakselis, Grade 6
Hoffman Estates, Illinois**

Ramona Quimby, Age 8

by Beverly Cleary

CHALLENGE/ COURAGE

FRIENDSHIP & FAMILY

HUMOR

I think that *Ramona Quimby, Age 8* is a terrific book because it is full of adventures that happen in an everyday life. Like the first day of third grade, or the first time riding a bus to school and feeling all grown up.

If you ever feel like you want to do more and make your own decisions, then this is the right book for you! Ramona is the kind of girl who has to deal with her mom going to work, her dad going to school, the car not starting, and having to get along with Willa Jean, a five-year-old, every day after school. If you like books that have adventure, courage, work, bad days, and exciting ones, then *Ramona Quimby, Age 8* is the book for you!!!

Ashley Baker, Grade 5
Fort Smith, Arkansas

Runaway Ralph

by Beverly Cleary

ADVENTURE

ANIMAL

HUMOR

Runaway Ralph is a wonderful book. It's about Ralph, a mouse with a motorcycle. Ralph wants to be free to do anything and eat peanut butter sandwiches until he drops. Instead, he gets trapped in a cage at Happy Acres Camp.

I like this book because it made me laugh, and it is full of funny songs and action. It is the kind of book that keeps you happy and entertained. This book reminds me of *The Mouse and the Motorcycle*.

It is very well illustrated. The illustrations are in black and white, but I don't care. I recommend this book to anyone who likes funny songs and funny lines. I think you should read this book.

Alex Campbell, Grade 5 ⋯⋯⋯
Cincinnati, Ohio

The Cat Who Went to Heaven

by Elizabeth Coatsworth

80 pages

Have you ever laughed at and felt sorry for someone at the same time? Elizabeth Coatsworth's *The Cat Who Went to Heaven* can make you feel that way. The story is really more about an artist than a cat, but the cat is very special.

One day, the artist gave his housekeeper one of his last silver coins to buy scraps to eat. She came back with a beautiful calico Japanese bobtail. At first, the artist did not like this creature, but then he remembered a legend that said that three-colored cats are good luck.

I really think that you should read this book to find out the very happy ending of this great story. I especially liked the songs of the housekeeper at the end of every chapter. Cat lovers might be disappointed at first because the title makes you think the book is only about a cat. But as you read it, you begin to feel the happiness and sadness of the artist, and you forget about the title.

Mary Elise Crawn-Vincent, Grade 4
Tallahassee, Florida

Sadako and the Thousand Paper Cranes

by Eleanor B. Coerr

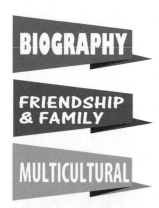

64 pages

This is a true story that took place in Japan after the atom bomb was dropped. Sadako was a little girl who got the disease called leukemia; they called it the atom bomb disease. When she was in the hospital, she started to make paper cranes. It was a legend that if a person who was sick could fold a thousand paper cranes, she would become well. Sadako made only 644 paper cranes before she died.

I loved the book. It was one of the best books I have ever read. It showed how this little girl had the courage to try to fold a thousand paper cranes so that she would become healed. She had so much faith that she would be okay.

Lisa Bondi, Grade 6
Matteson, Illinois

A Special Gift

Be sure to read the epilogue to *Sadako and the Thousand Paper Cranes*. An epilogue is located at the end of some books with extra information not found in the story. In this case, it tells of a very special gift given to Sadako by her friends and classmates.

Molly's Pilgrim

by Barbara Cohen

Molly's Pilgrim is a wonderful book about a little girl who moves to a new town. Molly has a hard time at her new school in Winter Hill. Other kids in her class laugh, sing mean songs, and make fun of her. Molly's feelings are hurt, and she doesn't like going to school. But all of a sudden, Molly starts to like school when her teacher gives them an unusual assignment. They have to make a pilgrim doll. If you want to find out why this assignment changes her feelings about her school, you'll have to read the book!

Kelly Wallace, Grade 6
Hadsonville, Michigan

Thank You, Jackie Robinson

by Barbara Cohen

Thank You, Jackie Robinson is a very adventurous book about a kid named Sam who is a total Dodger freak. I mean, he *loves* the Brooklyn Dodgers. It takes place in the year 1949. Sam and his mother live in the upstairs of an inn. Sam doesn't have a father, though, because he died a long time ago. Sam is very unusual because he can recite the events of any Dodger game played in the last five years. But every time he recites one to one of his friends, he never gets to finish it. Then Sam meets this really cool African-American guy named Davy, who is the new cook. Davy lets Sam think they will have a great friendship. Davy takes Sam to his first baseball game. Then they're always going to baseball games. But then Davy has a heart attack. I really think this is a great book. I think that this book is great for kids who feel strongly about other people.

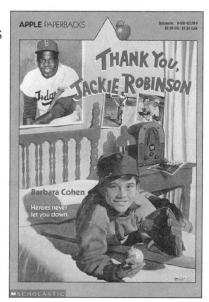

Carrie Holtgrefe, Grade 4
Cincinnati, Ohio

The Magic School Bus Inside the Earth

by Joanna Cole

ENVIRONMENT

FANTASY & FOLKLORE

HUMOR

When Joanna Cole and Bruce Degen made *The Magic School Bus Inside the Earth,* they must have had great imaginations. I sometimes wonder where they get their clever ideas, because who ever heard of a digging bus, a bus riding on an erupting volcano, and kids going to the center of the earth? Read this book because it's not only funny, but you learn science, too.

**Joey Dussault, Grade 5
Medford, Massachusetts**

Author! Illustrator!

Sometimes a writer and illustrator go together like cookies and milk. Or like magic and school buses! Bruce Degen's wacky cartoon-style illustrations, combined with Joanna Cole's informative texts, have conjured up one of the most successful science series ever. What do you think of other author-illustrator partnerships?

My Brother Sam Is Dead

by James L. Collier and Christopher Collier

CHALLENGE/ COURAGE

HISTORY

This book is a very good one for people who like to read historical fiction. It takes you on a roller-coaster ride because the story is so topsy-turvy. The Meeker family has a problem. Their rebellions son, Sam, is fighting in the Revolutionary War! The family seems different without Sam. They have more chores and are lonely and grumpy. Twelve-year-old Timothy, Sam's younger brother, is confused. Should he be headstrong like Sam, or should he stick with his loyal Tory family?

I like this book because it has suspense, lots of action, and descriptive language that made me feel like I was actually there watching it happen. It reminded me that all lives end somehow and that we all have different feelings and actions.

My Brother Sam Is Dead does not have illustrations, but you can picture what is going on in your mind. I recommend this book to anyone who likes to read chapter books, because it is very well written. Beware if you do not like action and danger. I have the feeling, though, that anyone who picks up this book will not be able to put it down.

**Kelly Jones, Grade 4
Leesburg, Virginia**

Cheetahs, the Swift Hunters

by Gladys Conklin

32 pages

Cheetahs, the Swift Hunters is a really good book. I like it because it shows how a cheetah grows up and how it learns to hunt.

The story starts out with a female cheetah looking for a mate. She finds a mate and has three babies. One of the babies dies because hyenas attack it. We get to see how the cubs grow up and learn to hunt. The cubs go along with their mother and watch her. When they get older, the cubs help her catch the prey. The story ends when the cubs are 18 months old and they go away to live by themselves.

The book is very exciting, and the artwork is very good. The pictures look like real cheetahs. I enjoyed reading this book, and I recommend it to you if you like cats or wild animals.

Ben Stillman, Grade 4
Lynnwood, Washington

Speed Limit 65 mph

Watch out if you're in the slow lane and a cheetah comes up behind you! Cheetahs can run as fast as 65 miles per hour. They are the fastest animals in the world.

Stonewords: A Ghost Story

by Pam Conrad

144 pages

I recommend this book to anyone who likes ghost stories. I also recommend it to people who like to go back in time. This book is about two girls who have the same name. One's name is Zoe. The other's name is Zoe Louise. The first time Zoe met Zoe Louise, Zoe was four years old. Zoe Louise was more than one hundred years old! From that day on, living in the same house separated by a staircase and a century, Zoe and Zoe Louise are an important and permanent part of each other's lives. Now Zoe is older and, although Zoe Louise never grows up, she is changing in dreadfully frightening ways!! Time is running out for Zoe's best friend—and she is the only one who can help her. To do so, she must travel back one hundred years and somehow alter the past.

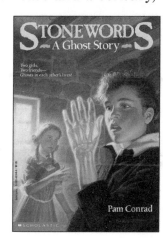

Mary Jane Thillen, Grade 4
Minneapolis, Minnesota

The Face on the Milk Carton

by Caroline B. Cooney

192 pages

CHALLENGE/COURAGE

DRAMA

ENVIRONMENT

MYSTERY

In *The Face on the Milk Carton,* Janie is perfectly happy with her parents until one lunch hour she and her friends are talking about the kidnapped-kid warnings on the back of milk cartons. Suddenly, Janie gets curious and looks on the back of her carton. She turns pale. That is her face on the carton! Could her loving parents, whom she adores, be kidnappers?

And why are there no pictures of her before she was five? She tells herself she is seeing things, but her face is still staring back at her from the carton. This is a heart-stopping chapter book that will turn your life upside down. Read how Janie and her friend Reeve unravel this twisted mystery.

Natasha Holstein, Grade 4
Houston, Texas

Goblins in the Castle

by Bruce Coville

176 pages

ADVENTURE

FANTASY & FOLKLORE

MYSTERY

Toad-in-a-Cage Castle was filled with secrets—secrets such as the hidden passages that led to every room, the long stairway that wound down to the dungeon, and the weird creature named Igor who lived there. But it was the mysterious night noises that bothered William the most—the strange moans that drifted through the castle where he was raised. He wanted to know what caused them. Then, one night, he found out . . .

I liked this story because William made a lot of new friends on his adventure! When I was reading the book, I had all of the feelings that you could think of! The pictures weren't in color, but they were neat! I recommend this book for all ages.

Brandy Nutter, Grade 3
Stanley Town, Virginia

My Teacher Fried My Brains

by Bruce Coville

THRILLS & CHILLS

SCIENCE FICTION

This book is about a boy trying to prevent an alien invasion. Duncan finds out that there's an alien who's dressed up like a human and posing as one of his teachers! The boy knows something is going on, but at first he doesn't realize who the alien is.

This book is well written and very adventurous, but it needs a better ending. The ending just leaves you behind.

Mayoora Rajgopal, Grade 5
Elmhurst, New York

Doing the Twist

Coville spices up ordinary teacher troubles by adding a twist: What might happen if the teacher were an alien? That's a good way to get started writing science fiction. Just take the plot of a realistic story you've read. Then change a character to an alien, or the setting to another planet. What happens?

My Teacher Fried My Brains

by Bruce Coville

THRILLS & CHILLS

SCIENCE FICTION

If you like science fiction, here is a book you might like! *My Teacher Fried My Brains* is about a kid named Duncan Dougal who gets his brains fried by his alien teacher. Guess what? He actually gets smarter by getting his brains fried! The best part in this story is when Duncan meets Krablin (his alien teacher). If you like this book, you should check out some of its exciting sequels, such as *My Teacher Is an Alien, My Teacher Glows in the Dark,* and *My Teacher Flunked the Planet.*

Author: Bruce Coville

Kevin Lee, Grade 4
East Brunswick, New Jersey

My Teacher Is an Alien

by Bruce Coville

My Teacher Is an Alien is about a teacher who gets captured by an alien. The alien substitutes for her class. But then Susan (the main character) sneaks into his house and discovers what the alien is up to. She gets a friend to help her prove that "Mr. Smith" is really an alien. The book made me feel like I was actually there and everything was happening to me. My favorite part was when Susan pretended to faint and held onto "Mr. Smith's" ear, trying to pull his mask off. The main character was sort of like me and one of my friends, Lauren, because she is not afraid to do things, but she doesn't really want to do them alone. That's why I like Susan. I like this book because I like exciting books. And the book left me thinking: Could my teacher be an alien, too?

**Leah Tibbetts, Grade 5
Amherst, New York**

Undying Glory: The Story of the Massachusetts 54th Regiment

by Clinton Cox

Undying Glory is an incredible true story. The book is about the first black regiment in the Civil War, the Massachusetts 54th, and its battle to be able to fight in the Civil War. At first, Governor Andrew of Massachusetts would not let the black men in the war. The Confederates warned the Union that if black soldiers fought and were captured, they would be returned to slavery. But the men did not care. They just wanted to fight for the North. Finally, Governor Andrew let them fight. The entire regiment was black except the leader, Colonel Robert Gould Shaw. The book also has photographs of people from the 54th Regiment, as well as pictures of monuments and famous black people in the war. The author wants us to know that black men were a factor in the Union defeating the Confederacy.

**Matt Shea, Grade 5
Oneonta, New York**

Battles to Fight

African Americans have served bravely in every war in this country from the American Revolution to the Gulf War. However, most of them could not serve beside their fellow white soldiers because the armed services were not integrated until 1948, after World War II. African-American units often had to make do with inferior supplies and conditions.

The Red Badge of Courage

by Stephen Crane

208 pages

ADVENTURE

CHALLENGE/ COURAGE

HISTORY

The story is about two boys fighting in the Civil War. The boys' names are Henry and Tom. This book tells about all the troubles and situations they get themselves into while being in the army.

I liked this book because it made me laugh at the funny things they did, and sad because so many people died in the war. This book also has pictures on every other page to show you what the story is about.

If you like lots of action, this is a great book for you.

Farrell Belknap III, Grade 3
Garrettsville, Ohio

Jurassic Park: The Junior Novelization

Screenplay by Michael Crichton and David Koepp, adapted by Gail Herman

96 pages

ADVENTURE

THRILLS & CHILLS

SCIENCE FICTION

Are you up for an exciting, action-packed story? Well, if you are, *Jurassic Park* is just the right book for you. The story takes place on a small island just off the coast of Costa Rica, San Jose. On this island, dinosaurs are being brought back to life through cloning; but through the greed of another company, the dinosaurs start running loose around the park. And if that isn't enough, three guests—Dr. Alan Grant, Lex, and her brother, Tim—are lost in the park. Can they bring the park under control before it's too late?

I liked this book because it has a lot of action and suspense in it. Also, most of all, it's believable. Unfortunately, there are some scenes in the book that are quite gory, like when the Dilophosaur slashes at Dennis Nedry's belly, spilling his intestines. Also there are a lot of technical words. Other than that, it's a great book. I recommend that you read this book, which is written by the author of *Rising Sun* and *Congo.* If you've seen the movie, you'll love the book.

Ted Yang, Grade 7
Taipei, Taiwan

Catherine, Called Birdy

by Karen Cushman

224 pages

ADVENTURE

FRIENDSHIP & FAMILY

HUMOR

This book is a great fiction story about a girl growing up in medieval times. Catherine is always locked up in her house learning the manners of a young lady while she sees children playing happily outside.

Catherine would love to be a crusader, peddler, painter, and maker of songs, but her mother and father think it's nonsense for a young lady to have a job like that.

When her Uncle George comes to visit her, he encourages Catherine to follow her dreams and do what's best for her. She thinks about running away from home and living with her brother at his monastery.

She also thinks about running away with a Jewish family that came to her house for protection from a dangerous storm. She would do anything to get out of her boring house!

Catherine has very exciting adventures that are a lot of fun reading about!

Kim Lawrence, Grade 6
Mentor, Ohio

Author! Author!

Karen Cushman says she has always learned everything from books. When she wanted to be a ballerina, it didn't occur to her to take a dance class. She checked out a library book! Her favorite advice for would-be writers? READ!

Santa Claus Doesn't Mop Floors

by Debbie Dadey and Marcia Jones

80 pages

ADVENTURE

FANTASY & FOLKLORE

MYSTERY

Santa Claus Doesn't Mop Floors is about the Bailey School's new janitor named Mr. Jolly. Mr. Jolly seems a lot like Santa. He's fat, he has a big white beard, and he keeps the school as cold as the North Pole. A lot of weird things happen in this book. Some kids think he is Santa Claus, and some don't. Whether you believe in Santa Claus or not, you might still enjoy reading this book to find out what makes Santa, I mean Mr. Jolly, so special.

Jason Norris, Grade 3
Mechanicsburg, Pennsylvania

The B. F. G.

by Roald Dahl

221 pages

ADVENTURE

FRIENDSHIP & FAMILY

HUMOR

In *The B.F.G.* there are ten giants: one good giant named The Big Friendly Giant (nicknamed B.F.G.) and nine bad giants.

I liked the book in the beginning because the B.F.G. was spreading good dreams to the children, which is a very nice thing to do, and he saw a girl staring at him. The B.F.G. picked up Sophie (that's her name) and took her to Giant Country so she couldn't tell people about him.

I also liked the middle, where the B.F.G. told Sophie about the nine bad giants. They like the people in different countries because of their flavors. For instance, people in Chile taste like chili, and people in Alaska taste like ice pops.

Author:
Roald Dahl

After hearing all this bad stuff, Sophie said, "Let's make a plan to get ride of the bad giants." That's what they do in the end, so you will have to read the book to find out what happens.

Christine Trontell, Grade 5
Lebanon, New Jersey

Charlie and the Chocolate Factory

by Roald Dahl

174 pages

ADVENTURE

CHALLENGE/ COURAGE

HUMOR

This book is about Charlie Bucket's miracle adventure in a chocolate factory. Charlie is a poor boy. Luckily, he found a dollar bill and bought a chocolate bar. The next minute, he was holding one of the five tickets to enter and learn the secrets of Mr. Wonka's fabulous chocolate factory and win a lifetime supply of Wonka's products. He is so lucky to journey through Wonka's factory. But Charlie must also be very careful of the perils of the world of Wonka, especially for the other four unloveable children who are joining him. Read the book to find out how the journey is, for the honest and kind, brave and true hero, Charlie.

I like this book very much because of Charlie's nice personality, the excitement of Charlie's adventure, and the happy ending. From the story, I learned that if you are honest, brave, and kind like Charlie, you can be somebody someday.

Jeffrey M. Lin, Grade 3
Flushing, New York

Danny, the Champion of the World

by Roald Dahl

208 pages

ADVENTURE

CHALLENGE/ COURAGE

CHALLENGE/ COURAGE

Danny, the Champion of the World is a very interesting book. It is about a boy who has a special relationship with his father. Danny and his father have a lot of fun together. They go fishing, fly kites, and ride fire balloons.

This book made me feel excited and reminds me of my dad, because he is very nice, just like Danny's father. I also like the artwork. I like the way the land and the birds are drawn. I also like the way the author puts just the right words into the story to give it a certain feeling. I think everyone would like this book, so I recommend it to all people who like to read.

Ben Norman, Grade 4
Great Falls, Virginia

If You Like the Book...

Roald Dahl's books have been made into some great films—*Willy Wonka and the Chocolate Factory, James and the Giant Peach, Matilda,* and *The Witches,* among others. It's interesting to see the changes involved as a story goes from the printed book to a moving picture on a screen. Dahl also wrote the screenplay for *Chitty Chitty Bang Bang.*

Esio Trot

by Roald Dahl

64 pages

CHALLENGE/ COURAGE

FRIENDSHIP & FAMILY

HUMOR

If you like comedy, romance, and turtles, you'll love to read *Esio Trot.* It is about Mr. Hoppy and Mrs. Silver. Shy Mr. Hoppy loves pretty Mrs. Silver but can't win her heart. Alfie, Mrs. Silver's turtle, gets all of the affection that Mr. Hoppy wants.

I recommend this book to children of all ages because you can read it again and again and never find it tiring. This book reminds me of my parents and my cats, because my father doesn't care for the cats, but my mom loves them.

The book's artwork is interesting. If you are a fast reader, slow down and take the time to find new things in the artwork.

I think the best part is the ending, because it is a happy ending. See how Mr. Hoppy changes not only his life but Mrs. Silver's, too. As I always say: Go ahead, turn the page!

Jennifer Schulz, Grade 4
Sterling, Virginia

The Giraffe and the Pelly and Me

by Roald Dahl

32 pages

ADVENTURE

FRIENDSHIP & FAMILY

HUMOR

This story is about a giraffe with a long neck, a pelican with a bucket-sized beak, and a dancing monkey. What else could they be but the Ladderless Window Cleaning Company? One day they get invited to clean all 677 windows belonging to the Duke of Hampshire himself! While they are cleaning the windows, they help capture a jewel thief.

This book was written by my favorite author, Roald Dahl, and it is filled with excitement and adventure. It made me laugh when I read the funny songs the monkey sang. Lots of things happen when the giraffe, the pelican and the monkey are together. This book is wonderful, and you should read it.

Christopher Dickie, Grade 4
Chula Vista, California

James and the Giant Peach

by Roald Dahl

112 pages

ADVENTURE

CHALLENGE/ COURAGE

FANTASY & FOLKLORE

FRIENDSHIP & FAMILY

You'll never believe how cool this book I read is! It's about this seven-year-old boy, James, who lived with the meanest, nastiest, and above all ugliest aunts in the world. One day, an old, weird man gives James special pellets that contain lots of power! All he has to do is put the pellets in water and drink them, and then he will have a wonderful life. But he falls, and all of the pellets come flying out of the bag. He tries to save them, but it's no use. They have already wiggled into the ground. The next day, something strange happens. A peach grows on the tree, but it doesn't stop until it's as big as a big house. That night, James goes out to look at the peach, and he notices a door near the bottom of the peach. When he goes in, he meets a big lady bug, a big centipede, a big spider, a big beetle, and an earthworm. They have a great time. I recommend this book to everyone who can read!

John Glynn, Grade 4
Longmeadow, Massachusetts

Illustrator! Illustrator!

Many of Roald Dahl's books were illustrated with Quentin Blake's zany pictures. Like many illustrators, Blake studied the work of cartoonists and tried to imitate their energetic, inventive look. He said his work took off when he realized "that because a drawing was going to be printed it didn't necessarily mean that it had to be well behaved."

Matilda

by Roald Dahl

240 pages

ADVENTURE

FRIENDSHIP & FAMILY

HUMOR

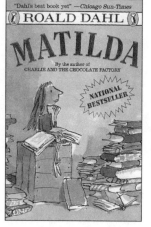

"Dahl's best book yet" —Chicago Sun-Times

ROALD DAHL

MATILDA

By the author of CHARLIE AND THE CHOCOLATE FACTORY

NATIONAL BESTSELLER

Matilda is a genius. Unfortunately, her parents treat her as if she were a fool. Her car salesman father and bingo-loving mother think that she is just an ordinary child, but they are wrong. With her great, brilliant mind, she makes up a few practical jokes to get back at her parents, and her parents don't stand a chance.

Miss Trunchbull, the mistress of Matilda's school, has terrorized generations of Crunchem Hall students, teachers, and parents. For example, ten-year-old Amanda Thripp had long golden pigtails in her hair, and pigtails are one thing Miss Trunchbull hates. So, Miss Trunchbull takes hold of Amanda's pigtails and swings her around and around. Then she lets go, and Amanda goes flying across the playground. When Miss Trunchbull goes after Miss Honey, Matilda's schoolteacher, she goes too far.

Read this stupendous story by Roald Dahl, pictures by Quentin Blake, to find out the fantastic way Matilda gets back at her parents and the terrible Miss Trunchbull.

Alyssa Juarez, Grade 4 · · · · · · · · ·
Laredo, Texas

The Witches

by Roald Dahl

208 pages

ADVENTURE

HUMOR

THRILLS & CHILLS

If you liked *James and the Giant Peach,* wait until you read *The Witches.* The Grand High Witch, the most powerful witch of all, makes up a formula to turn all of the children in the world into mice! My favorite part is when the grandson gets his revenge.

The World's Most Scrumdiddlyumptious Storyteller

ROALD DAHL

THE WITCHES

illustrated by Quentin Blake

This book reminded me of how bad the world can be sometimes. It sometimes made my stomach feel sick, like when they listed the names of all the ingredients in the secret formula. The artwork is simple, but funny. I recommend this book to anyone, especially if you like fiction.

Bonnie June Jones, Grade 4
Sterling, Virginia

The Terrible Wave

by Marden Dahlstedt

125 pages

CHALLENGE/ COURAGE

HISTORY

THRILLS & CHILLS

Imagine being stranded on a mattress, floating above water! That happened to Megan Maxwell when the South Fork Dam broke. She was lost and on her own in her hometown of Johnstown, Pennsylvania. She had no one to protect her. I liked the part when the water began to rise, because I was scared that the wave would knock the house down. This book made me sad because 2,000 people died, and I know it really happened. This book reminds me of the earthquake in Japan that happened on January 17, 1995, that killed over 3,000 people. I recommend this book because it is exciting.

Michael Shultz, Grade 4
East Brunswick, New Jersey

Disaster!

Johnstown, Pennsylvania, has suffered many floods, big and small. But the worst was when the South Fork Dam above the town burst in 1889. Lake Conemaugh, emptied in just 35–45 minutes! A wave of water as high as a seven-story building swept down into Johnstown. Why did the dam break? Read and find out!

If You're Not Here, Please Raise Your Hand: Poems About School

by Kalli Dakos

64 pages

HUMOR

POETRY

Do you like school poems? If you do, then this is the book for you. This book is by a teacher named Kalli Dakos. The teacher got her ideas for the 60 funny poems from the students around her school. She made up funny stories about make-believe students and the scary and funny things that happened to them.

The thing I like the most about this book is the illustrations. They have lots of detail. One of my favorite illustrations is with the poem "I Brought a Worm." The picture showed a happy girl holding a worm. She ate the worm. The poem had a surprise ending—it was a candy worm! There was nothing about this book that I did not like.

I recommend this book for children of all ages and adults who like poems. I know I sure do!

Katie Molloy, Grade 4
Winchester, Massachusetts

The Courage of Sarah Noble

by Alice Dalgliesh

64 pages

CHALLENGE/
COURAGE

FRIENDSHIP
& FAMILY

HISTORY

The Courage of Sarah Noble is a delightful and beautiful story of an eight-year-old who journeys with her father in the wilderness of Connecticut in 1707. Sarah went with her father to cook for him while he built their first home.

I especially liked this story because of the faith, courage, and friendship of Sarah. It lets us know how Sarah dealt with the Indian children and was always friendly to them.

After building their home, Sarah's father left her with Tall John and his Indian family while he went back to fetch her mother, brothers, and sisters. At first, Sarah was afraid of Tall John and his squaw, but in time, they all fell in love with each other.

Read this book! It's a thrilling story of how Sarah blends into the Indian Culture.

**Amanda R. Baker, Grade 3
South Bend, Indiana**

Check It Out!

Like *The Courage of Sarah Noble, The Sign of the Beaver* by Elizabeth George Speare tells the true story of a colonial child left alone in the wilderness who found help from Native Americans. If you want to find out how both kids survived without their families, head to the nearest bookstore or library!

Little Sister

by Kathleen Daly

24 pages

CHALLENGE/
COURAGE

FRIENDSHIP
& FAMILY

Liz and her brother, David, go on a vacation to a tropical island. Liz's brother meets some friends named Sue and Peter. Liz gets left out and hurt feelings. Later, Liz saves a baby and gets a sea urchin stuck to her foot! To find out what happens next, read the book!! *Little Sister* is a good book for people who like the seashore and learning about it. I felt sad when Liz got a sea urchin in her foot and when David, Peter, and Sue wouldn't let her play. I think you will enjoy the book. It reminded me of how my sister gets to me. I like the way the illustrator put in details and used bright colors. The artwork is beautiful!

**Carolyn Quelly, Grade 2
Quakertown, Pennsylvania**

Amber Brown Is Not a Crayon

by Paula Danzinger

80 pages

CHALLENGE/COURAGE

FRIENDSHIP & FAMILY

HUMOR

I just read *Amber Brown Is Not a Crayon*! It's one of my favorite books. This book is about a girl named Amber Brown fighting with her best friend. Believe me, fighting with your best friend is no fun. But anyway, my favorite part is the end. The end is somewhat happy and sad. I was surprised about what happened, because Amber Brown and Justin were the best of friends. But I'm sure you'll like it, too. I recommend this book for ages 7–12 because it's a chapter book, and I think first graders are a little too young.

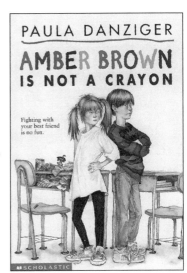

**Jenna Marie Gerbino, Grade 2
Port Jefferson, New York**

What's in a Name?

Amber Brown stands out partly because of her name. Do you know a Rose Bush or a Will Kall? Or maybe you've heard of someone whose name and job match, like a Dr. Pill, or a seamstress named Ms. Thread. Many writers keep lists of interesting names. Why not start your own list?

Spiderwebs to Skyscrapers: The Science of Structures

by Dr. David Darling

60 pages

ENVIRONMENT

This nonfiction book is about structures such as houses, bridges, spiderwebs, and birds' nests. It tells which shapes and materials are best suited to build them. It also has experiments to help you understand the facts.

The book has some interesting facts and nice big photos, but there are too many pictures and experiments and not enough reading. Also, some of the drawings and text are hard to understand.

**Patrick Bitonti, Grade 6
Kings Mills, Ohio**

Starfleet Academy: Worf's First Adventure

by Peter David

119 pages

ADVENTURE

FRIENDSHIP & FAMILY

SCIENCE FICTION

Worf and Simon boarded a shuttlecraft headed for Starfleet Academy and met Soleta, Zak, and Mark. They were all to enter the academy as cadets. At the academy, Zak and Worf got into a big fight as a result of Zak's prejudice toward Klingons. They both got sent to the Commanding Officer and were forced to be roommates as a punishment.

Later in the week, they all go on an old space station. Suddenly . . . WARBIRD ATTACK!!! A Romulan warbird fired at the station, knocking Zak into an empty shaft, but Worf and Soleta rescued him. Mark fired the phasers and, in response, the warbird rammed the station!

Luckily, it was only a test attack. All the cadets got A-pluses on their knowledge, bravery, and battle skills. This event was the beginning of Worf and Zak getting along better despite their ongoing differences.

I liked this book and recommend it to other fifth and sixth graders. It is filled with action and suspense. It also addresses the problems with differences, especially about being prejudiced toward others and how it affects relationships negatively. The book teaches how prejudices can be overcome through keeping an open mind.

Adam Sajdak, Grade 6
Depew, New York

Frederick Douglass Fights for Freedom

by Margaret Davidson

80 pages

BIOGRAPHY

CHALLENGE/ COURAGE

HISTORY

Does slavery mean cruelty? In *Frederick Douglass Fights for Freedom* it does. This book is based on the life of a man named Frederick Douglass who was a runaway slave from the South. I recommend this book to people with a caring heart because this book will make you cry. If you want to know more about what happened to Frederick, then read this book. You can take it from me, you won't be disappointed.

Eric J. Klein, Grade 4
West Harrison, New York

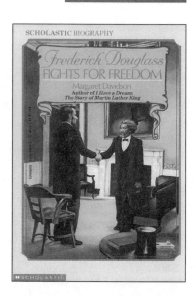

Helen Keller

by Margaret Davidson

BIOGRAPHY

CHALLENGE/ COURAGE

96 pages

Helen Keller was born a healthy baby. The she came down with a deadly sickness. No one thought she would recover. Surprisingly, she did recover, but she was not okay. She was blind. Later, they found out that she was deaf, too. She grew up knowing nothing about her surroundings. Her parents decided she needed help. A lady from Perkins Institution came. Her name was Annie Sullivan. She helped Helen, and while doing that, developed an unbreakable friendship.

This is an interesting, enjoyable book. It contains great details. I recommend it to anyone who likes to read biography or autobiography. Helen did amazing things and became famous. Learn what happens to a girl who became blind and deaf at a young age—read this moving book!

**Christina Delling, Grade 6
Lapeer, Michigan**

Check It Out!

Helen Keller overcame tremendous challenges, guided by the love and discipline of her remarkable teacher, Annie Sullivan. Margaret Davidson has written a biography of Sullivan that reveals how she faced her own challenges as well. Read *Helen Keller's Teacher* to learn more about Annie Sullivan's inspirational life.

Nothing's Fair in Fifth Grade

by Barthe DeClements

CHALLENGE/ COURAGE

FRIENDSHIP & FAMILY

144 pages

This book is about four girls: Jennifer, Elsie, Diane, and Sharon. Elsie is the new girl, and she is very fat. These girls have amazing and scary adventures that make your brain's wheels start turning fast.

It made me sad when they teased Elsie because of her weight. This book also made my heart beat so fast I felt like it was going to pop out. I hate to stop reading when I'm at a good part of the story.

This book taught me not to laugh at people no matter what their weight might be. It also taught me not to get angry for no reason like Elsie's mom did. These are very important lessons for me and anyone else who reads this book.

I recommend this book to any fifth grade student. If you read it I think you will really enjoy it. Take the chance.

**Erica Lessard, Grade 5
Port Jefferson, New York**

Book Body Connection

Does your heart beat faster like Erica Lessard's at a book's good parts? When you read something exciting, funny, or sad, your heart rate, muscle tension, and even brain chemistry undergo changes. Many scientists believe these effects can be good for you. So, get reading—and get healthy!

Robinson Crusoe

by Daniel Defoe

ADVENTURE

CHALLENGE/ COURAGE

DRAMA

288 pages

I really enjoyed *Robinson Crusoe*. It is a survival fiction book that takes place in the seventeen hundreds. Robinson Crusoe is a young man who tries to seek new lands by sailing to foreign places. Robinson Crusoe's ship sinks, and out of all the men on his ship he is the only survivor. How Robinson Crusoe survives I will leave up to you to find out.

Daniel Defoe did a great job writing this book. He gets into every detail so there isn't a part of the book you will not understand. If you are interested in adventure, excitement, and voyages, then I suggest this book to you.

Susan Goldstein, Grade 5
Port Jefferson, New York

Storytelling

Want to make a story you love come alive? Try telling it! To get started:

1. **Choose the right story.** Fairy tales, fables, and your own stories are good.
2. **Dramatize.** Use sound effects, "voices," gestures, props.
3. **Rehearse.** Use a mirror, tape recorder, and practice audiences.
4. **Start telling!** For more help, read *The Storyteller's Start-up Book* by Margaret Read MacDonald.

Nelson Mandela: "No Easy Walk to Freedom"

by Barry Denenberg

BIOGRAPHY

CHALLENGE/ COURAGE

160 pages

This is a detailed, interesting, and fantastic biography of Nelson Mandela. Some parts of the book were hard to understand and boring. But most parts were very interesting to read about. I liked learning about Mandela's life and the problems he faced. The book also tells a lot about the other blacks' problems and how they tried to stop the whites in South Africa from taking over. I strongly recommend this book to anyone who is interested in trying to make a difference.

Harmony Stempel, Grade 5
Rhinebeck, New York

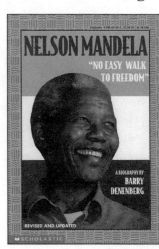

Stealing Home: The Story of Jackie Robinson

by Barry Denenberg

128 pages

Stealing Home is a great book. About forty years ago, Jackie, along with the rest of his team, took to the field. Some people cheered, some people booed, some people even threatened to kill him. Jackie Robinson still didn't give up, even though he was the first black man to play with the white men in the major leagues. This is a great book because Jackie Robinson stood up and fought for human rights on and off the diamond.

Kyle Williamson, Grade 5
Perrysburg, Ohio

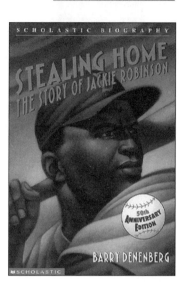

The Borderline Case

by Franklin W. Dixon

149 pages

The Borderline Case is a heart-pounding adventure. In this exciting story, two teenage boys, the Hardys, travel to ancient Greece on a student exchange program. It starts out as a normal trip, but later on it turns into a perilous journey. While on this trip, the boys get involved with a group of secret agents known as "The Network."

This story can be a little grotesque, so I recommend it to kids over eight years old. If you like action and exciting series books, you'll love this thrilling story!

Michael Dell, Grade 4
Great Falls, Virginia

Idea Factory

Q. Where do writers get their ideas?
A. Everywhere!
Serious writers keep idea files or notebooks. You can, too. Get a pack of 3-by-5 notecards or a notebook small enough to carry with you everywhere. Whenever you come across something interesting—that you've read, thought, overheard, seen—write it down. Immediately!

Morning Girl

by Michael Dorris

CHALLENGE/ COURAGE

HISTORY

This book is about this girl whose parents call her Morning Girl. She loves the beach. She gets up early every day to swim. Her parents say that she never takes any time to relax. The book talks about all the things she does. At school, the kids make fun of her name. They make fun of her because she is always busy. But she doesn't care. She just does what she wants. She is like me in a way. She is busy swimming and I am busy with ballet. I love ballet, and some people just don't understand how anyone would want to go to ballet all the time. This is a good book for people to read, so that they can realize some people are happy with what they do. They don't have to be in a group all the time. I give this book five stars!

**Alexandria Maiocco, Grade 4
Medford, Massachusetts**

Top Five Ways to Find a Good Book

5. Read book review.
4. Read over someone's shoulder. (But don't let him or her catch you!)
3. Check out the award winners at the library or bookstore.
2. Ask a friend, parent, librarian, or teacher.
1. Read this book!

This Is My House

by Arthur Dorros

ENVIRONMENT

This Is My House is a truly exciting book because it tells about a lot of different houses in the world. There are houses of many shapes and sizes. I learned that all over the world, there are many different houses, but they are still called home. Houses are extremely important because they protect us and keep us warm. You can make a home out of cardboard, wood, animal hide, or a cave. You can even live in a car.

The artwork was nice and colorful. I enjoyed it very much. This book made me think that we are awfully lucky to live in a real home instead of living out in the street.

**Mireya Ruiz, Grade 5
Denton, Texas**

Jacob's Rescue, A Holocaust Story

by Malka Drucker and Michael Halperin

128 pages

CHALLENGE/ COURAGE

HISTORY

This is one of my favorite books because it tells about the bravery of a young boy during the Holocaust. The book is about a boy named Jacob who must leave his home and family, and live with strangers in order to hide from the Nazis. This is a true story. After I read this book, it made me think about how people survived the Holocaust. It also showed how some people risked their lives to help other people. I think everyone should read this book to learn more about the Holocaust so terrible things like this will never happen again.

Daniel Janoff, Grade 5
Cherry Hill, New Jersey

The Twenty-One Balloons

by William Pène DuBois

184 pages

ADVENTURE

ENVIRONMENT

SCIENCE FICTION

The main character of this incredible book is a schoolteacher named Professor Sherman. When Professor Sherman retires, he decides to live in a hot-air balloon because it will be peaceful and quiet. (Or so he thinks!)

But Professor Sherman runs into a little problem. You see, a seagull pops his balloon when he happens to be floating over the island of Krakatoa, where a volcanic eruption happens to be in progress. Will the professor find a way to escape the disaster? I'm not going to tell you— read the book to find out!

One of the fun things I learned from this book was how long hot-air balloons can stay in the air. I liked the artwork because it let me see what the writer was thinking. I feel like I got to peek inside his imagination.

This book reminds of *Journey to the Centre of the Earth* because they are both about amazing places. They both have lots of action and they both have volcanoes. Plus, they both have a main character who loves adventure. . . just like me!

John Jozef, Grade 6
Port Jefferson, New York

The Math Wiz

by Betsy Duffey

80 pages

I like this book because I'm interested in sports and I want to learn more about people who are good at different things. I learned how it feels when you're good at math and not at sports or anything else. Plus, I learned that there's always a friend out there for you.

This book is about a boy named Marty. He is a math wiz, and when he has gym, he's always picked last for teams. When he's in gym, he always thinks different things like this: "Math Wiz + P.E. = Misery" and "Math Wiz – P.E. = ?????." So to find out more about Marty, put your eyes to the book and READ!!

Chrissy Schneider, Grade 5
Appleton, Wisconsin

Check It Out!

Kids who like sports or horses can find lots of stories with characters who share their interests. Kids who like math or science may find it harder. Here are some good books to try: *Math Curse* by Jon Scieszka and Lane Smith, and the *Einstein Anderson, Science Sleuth* series by Seymour Simon.

Forward Pass

by Thomas J. Dygard

192 pages

I liked this book because, first of all, it's about an issue that troubles America today: Should girls be allowed to play football? This realistic novel made me think about this issue. Another reason I liked this book is that it's packed with problems that just get worse and worse. One of the problems is that Jill's parents, at first, don't want Jill to play football. The reason the coach wants Jill on the team is that Aldridge High's football team is sorry, and Jill can catch better than all of Aldridge High's receivers put together. Will Jill get to play football or not? Read and find out! This book is for the sports fanatic in all of us.

Derek J. Avery, Grade 5
Houston, Texas

Sam and the Firefly

by P. D. Eastman

72 pages

ADVENTURE

HUMOR

This cool book is about a firefly that gets in big trouble because he confuses everybody. This firefly can write words, and once he wrote "stop" on the highway, causing cars to crash. The artwork is bright, and the firefly's words are brilliant. The fireflies remind me of flashing lights. I liked the book because the firefly is mischievous and the owl is helping to straighten him out. The character Sam the owl kept the firefly out of trouble. I recommend this book to others who like animal stories.

Casey Bender, Grade 4
Partage, Wisconsin

Shared Reading

There's nothing like a great book—except sharing it! Here's how:

1. **Read aloud.** Make it part of your family's daily routine.
2. **Start a book discussion group.** Ask a librarian or teacher to help.
3. **Read to someone who can't.** Check out *The Kid's Guide to Service Projects* by Barbara Lewis to find an audience who will appreciate a reader.

Gone-Away Lake

by Elizabeth Enright

256 pages

ENVIRONMENT

FRIENDSHIP & FAMILY

This book is about a girl named Portia, her brother, Foster, and her cousin, Julian. Portia and Foster are from the city, and every summer they go to Julian's house in the country. They always have fun, but this year Julian and his family bought a new house with unexplored land all around. Julian is a nature freak, and so one day he and Portia go exploring and find something special. "Let's keep this a secret for a while," Portia said. Read this book and I'm sure you'll enjoy finding out Portia's and Julian's "secret." If you're like me and never want this book to end, there's a great sequel to it: *Return to Gone-Away.*

Patrick Cacchio, Grade 5
Rhinebeck, New York

Author! Author!

Elizabeth Enright began her career as an illustrator. Then one day she wrote a story to go along with some of her drawings. Book critics liked her story better than her pictures. She began writing and illustrating, but eventually her books were illustrated by others.

America's Children

selected by Linda Etkin and Bebe Willoughby `96 pages`

BIOGRAPHY

FRIENDSHIP & FAMILY

HISTORY

POETRY

America's Children is a book about children, for children. It has stories, poems, and letters that tell about growing up in America. There are stories about colonial days, growing up during World War I and II, and about the 1960s and 1970s. These stories tell what life was like and describe thoughts and feelings that the children had. I like this book because I am interested in the experiences that children had in the past and what children were like in America many years ago.

Here are a few of my favorites:

"My Trip to the World's Fair, 1939" is about a girl who went to the World's Fair with her father, where there was food from around the world and things of the future. It was so big she thought her father wouldn't know the way back. I would like to have gone to the World's Fair!

I also loved "Crew Cut." A boy growing up in the 1950s had a terrible cowlick problem. He wanted a new haircut but his parents said "NO." Usually, boys got crew cuts during the summer. But this boy was never allowed to. I felt really bad for him when I read this story.

I recommend this book because it is full of interesting stories about children, and also because it is full of historical facts. I learned a lot while reading this book, and I know you'll like it too!

John Connors, Grade 4
Medford, Massachusetts

Aliens for Breakfast

by Jonathan Etra and Stephanie Spinner `64 pages`

ADVENTURE

FANTASY & FOLKLORE

MYSTERY

SCIENCE FICTION

Aliens for Breakfast is about a boy who was getting ready to eat his breakfast when an alien came out of his cereal. The alien told the boy about the bad Dranes and how they destroyed planets. The alien asked if the boy could help him destroy the Dranes and save Earth. "Dranes can turn into anything they want to," the alien told the boy. A Drane came to Earth two days ago, and a new boy started school two days ago. Why is everyone copying this new kid?

Solve the mystery—read *Aliens for Breakfast*.

Rachel Vento, Grade 4
Parker, Colorado

Eleanor Roosevelt: First Lady of the World

by Doris Faber

64 pages

This book was very interesting. It was detailed and very accurate and enjoyable. Eleanor's life was quite interesting. The book was never boring, and I kept coming back to it. I never knew anyone could live through some of the things Eleanor did. I found it hard to believe that anyone could be so active and interesting. She was a hard worker and never quit, even after her husband passed away. Her nickname suited her well. I recommend this book to people who work very hard. Eleanor was not considered a quitter.

Chrissy Couser, Grade 5
Rhinebeck, New York

Bury My Bones, But Keep My Words: African Tales for Retelling

retold by Tony Fairman

192 pages

Bury My Bones, But Keep My Words is a collection of African folktales. This book gave me a good feeling for life in Africa. It had a variety of African vocabulary, using such words as *omutugwa, igasi yi hano,* and *fani wi.*

Some of the stories are very close to American stories. For example, "Omutugwa" is almost the exact same story as "Cinderella." The only difference is that when the two stepsisters try on the slipper, they cut off their heels and their toes to try and make it fit.

The illustrations by Meshack Asare have a very African feel to them. They bring the book to life.

I think the author of this book wanted to let everyone get a bit of African culture. I also think he loves hearing, sharing, and making up stories. I enjoyed this book because it is different from the stories I usually hear. There is a variety; some of them are funny, some scary, and some have morals.

Michael Fidrych, Grade 5
St. Augustine, Florida

White Fang II: Myths of the White Wolf

by Elizabeth Faucher

184 pages

Do you like animals in adventures? I do! That's why I liked *White Fang II: Myth of the White Wolf.* It's based on the movie. It's about a young man named Henry Casey and his loyal wolf, White Fang. Gold fever has taken over his life, until he meets a young Haida woman named Lily. Henry finally starts to question his old ways. The Haida tribe is starving. The chief, Moses Joseph, has dreamed that a white wolf will lead his tribe to food. To find out what happens next, read the book. I recommend this book to people who love adventures.

**Dustin Smith, Grade 4
Whittemore, Iowa**

Lost on a Mountain in Maine

by Donn Fendler

125 pages

This book is about a twelve-year-old boy named Donn Fendler who is hiking with his dad and brother. He gets impatient with them and heads down the mountain alone. It is foggy, and Donn loses sight of the trail. After that he spends ten days lost on the mountain in Maine.

On his way trying to find someone, he sees bears, owls, and other animals. Eating berries from bushes and hardly ever drinking from streams, he travels from 2 to 7 miles a day. The eighth day he finds abandoned cabins and stays there for the night. Then he finally gets rescued.

This is a true story. It is amazing that Donn went on such an adventure and remembered even the smallest details. With photographs instead of drawn pictures, it is an excellent book. To get even more information on the book, read it! Check out *Lost on a Mountain in Maine!*

**Dustin M. Briggs, Grade 4
San Diego, California**

Don't Get Lost!

Donn Fendler was lucky. He survived getting lost in the wilderness. Be safe—follow these tips when hiking or camping:

1. Always travel with a buddy.
2. Stick to marked trails.
3. Wear a whistle to blow if you get separated.
4. If you do get lost, hug a tree! Stay where you are.

Randall's Wall

by Carol Fenner

HUMOR

85 pages

If you like stories that are both sad and happy, then you should read *Randall's Wall*.

Randall's Wall is about a boy whose family is quite poor. He doesn't have any friends at school until he meets Jean Worth Neary, who changes Randall's life by being his first and only friend. Jean and Randall spend a lot of time together. The funniest time is after they go out to lunch. Jean took Randall to her house to take a bath because he was so dirty. He got in the bathtub with his clothes on, and the hamburger he had stuffed in his pocket floated to the top of the water!

This book is special to me because I really liked it, and because Carol Fenner, the author, wrote a letter to me.

Jenna Wegner, Grade 4
Kearney, Nebraska

Walking the Road to Freedom: A Story About Sojourner Truth

by Jeri Ferris

64 pages

Walking the Road to Freedom is an especially good book. It is a real-life story about Sojourner Truth and how she tried to stop slavery and help women get their rights. Sojourner Truth traveled a lot and could do almost anything a man could do. Run to the library and check it out!

Jeana Richards, Grade 3
Milwaukee, Wisconsin

Illustration Basics

Some tips for would-be illustrators:

1. **Learn to look.** Seeing how things really look is the heart of drawing well.
2. **Draw every day.** Most artists do.
3. **Experiment.** Try different ways of making lines, kinds of paint, scratchboard, photography, collage, print making.
4. **Examine books.** What do the illustrations add to the story? Try re-illustrating a book you love!

75

Zlata's Diary: A Child's Life in Sarajevo

by Zlata Filipovic

220 pages

BIOGRAPHY

CHALLENGE/COURAGE

MULTICULTURAL

You've probably heard of *Zlata's Diary*. It is a thirteen-year-old's diary with entries written during the war in Sarajevo. In the beginning, her diary was normal. She wrote about MTV, school, family, and friends.

A few months after her first entry, war broke out in Dubrovnik, a city near Sarajevo, Zlata's hometown. Pretty soon, the war spread to Sarajevo. Snipers went crazy and shot every moving figure. Bombs destroyed many houses and buildings. School was canceled because it was too dangerous. All of Zlata's friends either moved or were killed. Zlata was sad and lonely.

In many of Zlata's war entries, she wrote "I wish not to suffer the fate of Anne Frank."

Fortunately, Zlata's story has a happy ending. In December 1993, Zlata and her parents were taken to France, where they now live in peace. I think everybody will like this important book.

Serena Koepke, Grade 4
Schaumburg, Illinois

Put It in Writing!

Here's how to write a lively diary:

1. **Do "color commentary."** Don't just tell what happened. Include feelings, thoughts, and dreams.
2. **Be truthful and complete.** Write about negative experiences as well as happy ones.
3. **Write regularly.** Set aside a time at least once a week.
4. **Illustrate your diary.** Use photos, clippings, school papers, sketches, ticket stubs, pressed flowers, and more.

Harriet the Spy

by Louise Fitzhugh

304 pages

ADVENTURE

FRIENDSHIP & FAMILY

HUMOR

This is a funny, sad, and adventurous book about an eleven-year-old girl who wants to be a writer. But when she takes notes about her friends so she can write about them later, she isn't too careful about what she writes! One of the things she wrote was that "Carrie Andrews has an ugly pimple right next to her nose." And when she didn't know the name of a new boy, she gave him a name: "Boy with the purple socks!"

When her notebook gets in the wrong hands, her friends want to get revenge! Do they succeed? Read *Harriet the Spy*.

This is one book everybody will like!

Haley Drummond, Grade 4
Albuquerque, New Mexico

Generation Gap

When *Harriet the Spy* was published, many book reviewers disliked it. They felt Harriet was too spoiled and rude to be likable. Kids, however, loved the book, and it became a best-seller.

The Whipping Boy

by Sid Fleischman

96 pages

ADVENTURE

CHALLENGE/ COURAGE

FRIENDSHIP & FAMILY

HUMOR

The Whipping Boy is about two boys, Jemmy and Prince Brat. Jemmy is taken from an orphanage so he can be the whipping boy for Prince Brat. Because the prince is royalty, he cannot be punished for his wrongdoings. Jemmy must obtain all his punishments for him. And that he does, as the prince intentionally gets in trouble so Jemmy will get punished.

When Jemmy has had enough, he runs away, as does Prince Brat. It is then that their friendship grows. After a few days, the king puts up a reward for their capture. Two men named Hold Your Nose Billy and Cutwater are determined to find them. Learn how the prince and Jemmy put their friendship to the test in *The Whipping Boy*.

**Donald Epifano, Grade 5
Trumbull, Connecticut**

Wanted: Child to Punish

List this one under "Jobs to Avoid." Sid Fleischman made up his story *The Whipping Boy*, but he based it on a fact: Long ago, there really were servants whose job it was to be spanked when their child masters misbehaved!

Squanto: A Warrior's Tale

adapted by Ron Fontes and Justine Korman from the screenplay by Darlene Craviotto

32 pages

ADVENTURE

CHALLENGE/ COURAGE

HISTORY

MULTICULTURAL

Squanto: A Warrior's Tale is about a Native American named Squanto. The story is an adventure that starts when Squanto is captured and taken to England to be a slave. He escapes from his captors and then is found by monks. In the two years that he is away, he faces many dangers and also learns a lot from the white man. He learns an important lesson about prejudice. He finds out that there are good people even among the white men who captured him. Finally, he returns home after two winters. He is very, very happy to finally see his wife and tribe again.

If you like adventure, *Squanto* is a story that you will enjoy. I liked it because I am interested in Native Americans and their culture. The story is filled with facts about Native Americans.

**Albert Louis Trionfo, Grade 4
Vineland, New Jersey**

Monkey Island

by Paula Fox

160 pages

CHALLENGE/
COURAGE

FRIENDSHIP
& FAMILY

I really enjoyed *Monkey Island* by Paula Fox. She lives in Brooklyn, New York, which is close to where this book takes place.

Monkey Island is a sad book about a boy named Clay Garrity, whose parents abandon him. Clay finds two homeless people, Buddy and Calvin, who take care of him, but he wants to stay on the streets, so he might find his mom or dad.

I like Clay because he is brave and creative. He believes in himself and finds friends to live with, while looking for his mom and dad. He is creative enough to find food, a place to live, and people to trust.

Monkey Island is a good book. Read it to find out how Clay survives out on the streets. I bet you will enjoy it like I did.

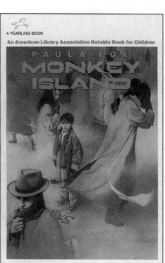

William A. Yokel, Grade 6
Indiana Hill, Ohio

The One-Eyed Cat

by Paula Fox

192 pages

ANIMAL

CHALLENGE/
COURAGE

FRIENDSHIP
& FAMILY

The One-Eyed Cat is about a boy named Ned. On his birthday, Ned is given a gun from his uncle. But his father, a minister, said that he couldn't have it until he was thirteen years old. Ned is eager to try it, so he disobeys his father and shoots it at night near the woods. After, Ned thinks that he may have shot a cat. But he isn't sure because he can only see a shadow in the dark. Ned doesn't think that he can tell anyone about what he has done or else he'll get into trouble. Ned ends up taking care of the injured cat and tells lots of lies doing so.

I think this book is great! It really gets its point across to all people: DO NOT LIE! If you do, you are going to have to remember all the lies that you make up, otherwise you'll get caught. That's what this book taught me.

Tamara Elwood, Grade 5
Oneonta, New York

The Slave Dancer

by Paula Fox

ADVENTURE

CHALLENGE/ COURAGE

HISTORY

`128 pages`

I read a wonderful book, *The Slave Dancer* by Paula Fox. It is about a boy, Jessie, from New Orleans. One day, when his mother sends him out to buy candles, he is kidnapped and put on the slave ship *Moonlight.* On the ship he has many experiences and comes to know how awful life is for a slave, until one day, the ship is wrecked.

I think you should read this moving, exciting, and interesting book. The only thing I didn't like are the illustrations, because they're very dark and difficult to see.

Gabrielle Joyce, Grade 5 · · · · · · · ·
Snyder, New York

Anne Frank: The Diary of a Young Girl

by Anne Frank

BIOGRAPHY

CHALLENGE/ COURAGE

HISTORY

MULTICULTURAL

`256 pages`

"I hope I shall be able to confide in you completely, as I have never been able to do in anyone before." Those were the words of a young girl writing in her diary; a young girl named Anne Frank. She was a normal girl who lived a normal life until she was forced to go into hiding. Why? Because she was Jewish. Long ago, Jewish people were persecuted because of their religion.

This book tells her thoughts and feelings. It is the most touching book I have ever read and probably ever will. I highly recommend it and hope that you will consider reading it.

Jessica Diaz, Grade 6
Spencerport, New York

"In Spite of Everything...

...I still believe that people are really good at heart," wrote Anne Frank in her famous diary. Anne Frank died in a concentration camp. But her words live on, thanks to her father, who took up her desire to work for unity. Her diary has been translated into 55 languages! The Secret Annex still exists in Amsterdam, preserved as a museum.

Roommates

by Kathryne Galbraith

48 pages

FRIENDSHIP & FAMILY

If you have ever had to share a room with a brother or sister, this is the book for YOU!

One day, Mimi and Beth find out their mother is having a baby. The sisters have to share a room. Beth and Mimi get angry at each other, and they fight and make each other jealous. One day, Beth takes black tape and splits the room in half. She tells her sister, one half is mine and one half is yours.

Shared Reading

There's nothing like a great book—except sharing it! Here's how:

1. **Read aloud.** Make it part of your family's daily routine.
2. **Start a book discussion group.** Ask a librarian or teacher to help.
3. **Read to someone who can't.** Check out *The Kid's Guide to Service Projects* by Barbara Lewis to find an audience who will appreciate a reader.

Read this book and you'll know what to do with your brothers or sisters. I like this book because I have no brothers or sisters, and I want to know what it's like to have one.

**Jacqueline Williams, Grade 5
Ft. Madison, Iowa**

Stone Fox

by John Reynolds Gardiner

96 pages

ADVENTURE

ANIMAL

CHALLENGE/ COURAGE

One of the best books I have ever read is *Stone Fox*. It is about a young boy who lives with his grandpa, and he loves him a lot. But one day, his grandpa gets really sick and can't do anything for a while. So it is up to Willy to take care of their farm. Willy is determined to find a way to save his grandpa and the farm. Willy enters a dog racing contest, and the winner wins 75 dollars. Well, I can't tell you the end of it, but I hope you enjoy it as much as I did.

**Ryan Strong, Grade 6
Lily, Wisconsin**

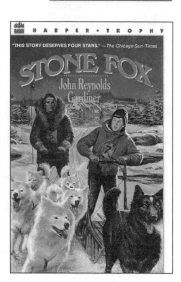

Family Pictures

by Carmen Lomas Garza

32 pages

FRIENDSHIP & FAMILY

MULTICULTURAL

Family Pictures is a great book about Carmen Lomas Garza's childhood. She tells little stories about growing up in Mexico. It has English at the top of its pages and Spanish at the bottom. If you know English, it can almost teach you Spanish, and if you know Spanish, it can almost teach you English. I know a little bit of Spanish myself. Adios!

Lakirsha Broussard, Grade 6
Houston, Texas

The Home Run Kings

by Clare and Frank Gault

80 pages

BIOGRAPHY

SPORTS

Starting with the Red Sox in 1914, and ending with the Yankees in 1935, Babe Ruth set more home run records than any other baseball player during that time. It was almost 40 years before Hank Aaron came along and broke the record for the most home runs in a career. This book is about the disappointments and pressures that went along with the glory of being a home run king.

I like baseball and learning statistics and facts about great baseball players. My father is a baseball trivia fanatic. After reading this book, I was able to tell him some interesting facts that even he did not know.

STAR REVIEW

Michael Fishman, Grade 6
Actor

Check It Out!

If you liked this book and it made you want to find out even more about a particular ballplayer, check out a series called *Baseball Legends*. The series includes biographies of about 33 of the game's greatest players, including, of course the Babe (under *Babe Ruth*).

Julie

by Jean Craighead George

240 pages

ADVENTURE

ANIMAL

CHALLENGE/
COURAGE

I loved *Julie,* the sequel to *Julie of the Wolves.* In the first book, we saw Julie survive the freezing cold, bleak tundra and live with wild wolves. Little did we know, her toughest challenge was yet to come.

In the sequel, Julie has to live with her father, Kapugen, his gussak wife, Ellen, and their baby, Amarog. If you think that sounds hard, just wait. Julie has to go back to the tundra and save her wolf pack. Why? Julie's father thinks Julie's wolves are going to attack his oxen because they need food, so he threatens to kill the wolves.

The race is on. Will Julie make it to the wolves before Kapugen kills them? If you want to find out, read this spine-tingling book.

**John Jones, Grade 5
Port Jefferson, New York**

Author! Author!

Jean Craighead George's great love of animals and nature shines through in all her books. In childhood, she spent plenty of time tromping in the outdoors, raising wild orphan animals, and even living off the land. Much later in life George spent a summer studying wolves in Alaska. This experience inspired the 1973 award-winning *Julie of the Wolves.*

My Side of the Mountain

by Jean Craighead George

176 pages

ADVENTURE

CHALLENGE/
COURAGE

ENVIRONMENT

FRIENDSHIP
& FAMILY

My Side of the Mountain is realistic fiction about a young boy named Sam Gribley. Most children I know can relate to this story.

Sam was the oldest of seven brothers and sisters. He got really angry at his parents and set off on a quest to find his great-grandfather Gribley's farm at the top of the Catskill Mountains.

I learned a lot from this book, like how to make a home in a tree, catch fish, trap deer, identify flora and fauna, and train and make friends with a hawk.

To find out what happens to Sam, read this book. Boys and girls alike will love this story!

**Beth-Ann Wilson, Grade 5
Copiague, New York**

Check It Out!

It took awhile—33 years to be exact—but George did write a sequel to the much-loved *My Side of the Mountain. My Side* (her first kids' novel) came out in 1959, and in 1990 *On the Far Side of the Mountain* was published, which continues Sam's outdoor adventures.

William and Boomer

by Lindsay Barrett George

24 pages

ANIMAL

FRIENDSHIP & FAMILY

This book is about a boy named William. One day, William goes fishing with his dad. He finds a baby goose, but he can't find its mom. Then, William takes the baby goose home and calls it Boomer.

Boomer follows William everywhere, but mostly to the lake. Boomer liked to swim, but William can't.

This story tells how William watches Boomer grow bigger and swim. One day, William is ready to try swimming himself.

I like this book because William likes the lake, fishing, turtles, and Boomer, just like I do. Having a goose for a pet would be fun!

Matt Evans, Grade 3 · · · · · · · · · · · ·
Sarasota, Florida

Indian Summer

by Barbara Girion

192 pages

FRIENDSHIP & FAMILY

MULTICULTURAL

If you were going on an Indian reservation, what would you expect? *Indian Summer* is a book about two girls who have two different cultures that are forced to live together for a month. Joni McCord from New Jersey expects teepees and head-dresses, but Sarah Birdsong, on the other hand, lives in a normal log cabin and dresses just like everyone else in the city. Sarah's friends on the reservation don't like the idea of outsiders living on their territory, and everything Joni says about her or her culture sends Sarah up in a rage. Can their similarities and differences bring them together to be friends? Read and discover the answer!

Rebecca Heilman, Grade 4
Houston, Texas

A Writer's Corner

Inspired to write? Make yourself a studio. Include:

1. **Desk and chair.** A clipboard and cushion will do.
2. **Paper.** All sorts, lined and unlined.
3. **Writing instruments.** Pens, pencils, a computer or word processor, if possible.
4. **Office supplies.** Paper clips, stapler, tape, glue stick, stamps, envelopes.
5. **Bulletin board.** Tack up ideas, quotes, pictures, anything to jump-start your creativity!

Koi and the Kola Nuts

by Brian Gleeson

40 pages

ANIMAL

FANTASY & FOLKLORE

FRIENDSHIP & FAMILY

MULTICULTURAL

Koi and the Kola Nuts is an African folktale about how one friend helps others and how this kindness is eventually repaid.

Koi is a young boy whose father, the chief, dies. Koi isn't treated like a chief's son anymore, so he sets off to find a new home where he will be treated like a chief's son. On the way, he helps several animals. The story continues with the animals helping Koi in his quest to find a village where he will be treated like a chief's son.

I like the colorful pictures that are drawn in red African designs. There is also an audiocassette that is narrated by Whoopi Goldberg.

If you like folktales, you'll like this book.

**Michelle Alexander Neads, Grade 5
Cincinnati, Ohio**

Teammates

by Peter Golenbock

32 pages

BIOGRAPHY

CHALLENGE/ COURAGE

HISTORY

SPORTS

Teammates is about Jackie Robinson and Pee Wee Reese. It taught me about the Negro leagues. The Negro leagues had extraordinary players, but they didn't get a lot of money. Laws against segregation didn't exist in the 1940s in many places in this country. They didn't even have baseball cards of black people.

Branch Rickey, the general manager of the Brooklyn Dodgers, wanted the best players he could find, regardless of their race. Rickey thought Jackie Robinson would be perfect because he was cool-headed and a great, great player. But it was a lot of pressure for Jackie. If he disgraced himself on the field, the other players would use it as an excuse to keep blacks off the team.

Jackie had to face abuse throughout the season. When some teammates wanted to kick Jackie off the team, Pee Wee Reese said that he didn't care if he was black, blue, or striped. He is a player who can help us, and that's what counts. Jackie and Pee Wee Reese become great friends.

I liked the story because I like baseball.

**Shane Vanderbilt, Grade 5
Lauista, Nebraska**

Check It Out!

The library has many books about Jackie Robinson and the Negro Leagues. Two good books are *Jackie Robinson: He Was the First* by David Adler, and *Shadowball: The History of the Negro Leagues* by Geoffrey C. Ward.

The Legend of Jimmy Spoon

by Kristiana Gregory

180 pages

ADVENTURE

CHALLENGE/ COURAGE

MULTICULTURAL

I recommend *The Legend of Jimmy Spoon*. This book made me feel sad because Jimmy ran away and left his mom with five babies and his dad. I liked Jimmy because he liked adventure, and I do, too. I liked the artwork because it shows real detail in the pictures. If I could change something in the book, I would have had Jimmy fight in the war. He wasn't in it because Old Mother didn't want him to be killed like her two other sons (Old Mother is Jimmy's Indian mother and the chief's mother). A fun fact about this book is how Indians cooked and made medicines. There is a lesson to learn in this book, and it is never to run away from home. Read this book and find out how Jimmy survives.

**Lauren Fre, Grade 4
Ashland, Ohio**

Dolphin Adventure: A True Story

by Wayne Grover

48 pages

ANIMAL

DRAMA

ENVIRONMENT

If you like the ocean and you like animals, especially dolphins, you will go for this book. It is a true story about a diver named Wayne Grover who finds a family of dolphins 80 feet below the ocean surface. He realizes that one of the dolphins is bleeding and needs help. Will Wayne save the dolphin?

This book is really adventurous, and when I finished a chapter, I wanted to read the next one. The titles of the chapters are very interesting, like "Surgery on the Sea Floor." This book made me want to see wild dolphins just like Wayne did.

If you like wonderful books that you can read in one night, this is a book for you. I loved this book and I hope you do too!

**Crissa Nelson, Grade 3
Lynnwood, Washington**

Close Encounters of a Dolphin Kind

Did you know that swimming with wild dolphins is possible? In recent years, quite a few "dolphin encounter" businesses have blossomed. They take people out to special areas where the customers can pet, swim, or dive with dolphins. If you're ever in Florida or Hawaii, ask a tourism office for information.

Dinotopia

by James Gurney

160 pages

ADVENTURE

ENVIRONMENT

FANTASY & FOLKLORE

Dinotopia tells of a scientist and his son who are shipwrecked on an island where men and dinosaurs live together. It reminds me of the movie *Jurassic Park,* except in *Dinotopia* they live in peace. If you like dinosaurs, you'll love this book! The pictures are great. They make it into an adventure. This is one exciting book. After we read it in class, we all wanted to start over and read it again.

Bradie Nielsen, Grade 3
Ephraim, Utah

Dinotopia

by James Gurney

160 pages

ADVENTURE

ENVIRONMENT

FANTASY & FOLKLORE

Dinotopia is an interesting book. It takes place in the nineteen hundreds on an undiscovered island that is inhabited by dinosaurs and humans, who live together in harmony. The main characters are Arthur Denison, his son, Will Denison, Bix (a Protoceratops), and Sylvia (a Dinotopian native). I like all of the main characters, especially Bix, because she can speak English and a ton of other languages. I like this book so much that I have read it seven times. Anybody who likes dinosaurs (or not) is sure to like this book and its illustrations. I think this book is one of a kind. This book leaves you wondering about the characters and what they will do next. It would be nice if James Gurney wrote a sequel to this book. How about it, Mr. Gurney?

Neal Riebel, Grade 6
Bay Village, Ohio

Author! Author!

James Gurney does careful research for his stories and illustrations. "I don't see myself as having created *Dinotopia*," he says, "because it feels like it existed before I discovered it. I'm just an explorer. Every morning, I put on my safari hat, head upstairs to the studio, and take a little adventure."

Shaquille O'Neal: Basketball Sensation

by Bill Gutman

48 pages

BIOGRAPHY

SPORTS

If you like slammin' action with big Shaquille O'Neal, this is the book for you! Did you know that the name Shaquille means little warrior? Of course you know that Shaquille isn't little anymore, because he is seven foot three, three hundred five pounds! This book includes real photos of him playing and of trophies that he won. The book tells how he had to travel and how he had a hard life. Shaq plays for the Orlando Magics, and in his rookie season he averaged 23 points per game. Shaq was rookie of the year in the 1992–1993 season. So if you had to describe Shaq in one word, you would say he's big!

Matt Chambers, Grade 4
Mahopac, New York

Shaq Attack!

Known for keeping his cool, a reporter once asked Shaquille O'Neal what gets him excited. He replied, "when my Mom tells me she loves me. That's the only thing I can think of!" Mrs. O'Neal, are you reading this? Also known for his sense of humor, O'Neal once convinced four of his teammates to dress up in wigs with him and present themselves as the "Shaqson Five."

A Story, A Story

by Gail E. Haley

36 pages

FANTASY & FOLKLORE

MULTICULTURAL

A Story, A Story is an African folktale. In it the Sky God owns all the stories in the world. A little old man named Ananse wants to buy the stories, but he has to retrieve three things. They are Osbeo, the leopard-of-the-terrible-teeth; Mmboro, the hornets-who-sting-like-fire; and Mmoatia, the fairy-whom-no-man-sees. Read and see if he gets the items and how. I like how tricky Ananse is and the things he is supposed to retrieve. The book made me feel like people should read it because it is exciting. The artwork in the book is neat. In order to make the pictures, they carved wood pictures and painted them with wet paint, then pressed the picture down on paper to print them. I recommend the book to others so they get to read stories about African people.

Katie Miller, Grade 3
Manteo, North Carolina

87

Here Comes Zelda Claus: And Other Holiday Disasters

by Lynn Hall

149 pages

ADVENTURE

FRIENDSHIP & FAMILY

HUMOR

Up on the housetop, reindeer pause. Out jumps good old...Zelda Claus? Who ever heard of a twelve-year-old dressing up as Santa Claus? You wouldn't believe how many scrapes Zelda Hammersmith gets into, including the one where she pretends to be a bell ringer for the Salvation Army. Every holiday she causes an unimaginable catastrophe, whether all alone or with the help of others. To find out what other humiliating pinches she gets herself into, read *Here Comes Zelda Claus*.

Lauren Wickline, Grade 5
Springfield, Ohio

Cousins

by Virginia Hamilton

128 pages

DRAMA

FRIENDSHIP & FAMILY

The book *Cousins* was highly recommended by my reading teacher, Mrs. Wilcoxson. It is about two girls, Patty Ann and Cammy, who always fight. I learned lots of lesson from this book. One: Don't always try to get your own way, because it can backfire. Two: Don't take people for granted or you will end up with a friend or two less. Three: Don't call people names, because it can hurt them. And four: Don't hate life, enjoy it. I liked this book because it is a real lesson-teacher. Why not read it yourself. Thanks, Mrs. Wilcoxson!

Melissa Duban, Grade 6
Stratford, Connecticut

Storytelling

Want to make a story you love come alive? Try telling it! To get started:

1. **Choose the right story.** Fairy tales, fables, and your own stories are good.
2. **Dramatize.** Use sound effects, "voices," gestures, props.
3. **Rehearse.** Use a mirror, tape recorder, and practice audiences.
4. **Start telling!** For more help, read *The Storyteller's Start-up Book* by Margaret Read MacDonald.

Outward Dreams: Black Inventors and Their Inventions

by Jim Haskins

128 pages

BIOGRAPHY

CHALLENGE/ COURAGE

HISTORY

This book is about African Americans who have made this world a better place. It tells about people such as Benjamin Banneker. He probably built the first clock made in America. The book also tells about inventors who never got any credit for their inventions. So if you like learning about the past as I do, read this book!

**Christopher Dyer, Grade 5
Fairburn, Georgia**

Author! Author!

Jim Haskins is one of America's most prolific nonfiction authors. He's written more than 110 books! When he was a young boy, he craved information and devoured a set of encyclopedias by age fourteen. His mother got them for him because he was an African-American child in Alabama in the 1940s and wasn't allowed in the public libraries.

Brighty of the Grand Canyon

by Marguerite Henry

224 pages

ANIMAL

FRIENDSHIP & FAMILY

HISTORY

Brighty was a smart young mule who lived in the Grand Canyon of Arizona. His original owner was murdered, but he passed through many other owners before finding the one who would help bring justice to his master. There are a few funny parts, but the most amazing thing about the story is that Brighty is just as smart as any person in the book! Plus, it's a true story.

**Annie Wilson, Grade 4
Sewickley, Pennsylvania**

Mama, Let's Dance

by Patricia Hermes

168 pages

Mama, Let's Dance is a touching book. In this book, three young children are abandoned first by their father and then their mama. They are forced to survive on their own. Will they stay together? Read and find out! This book made me feel sad for all the abused and neglected children in the world.

Amanda Griffin, Grade 7
Grove City, Pennsylvania

Author:
Patricia
Hermes

You Shouldn't Have To Say Good-bye

by Patricia Hermes

128 pages

If you like sad books like I do, this book is for you! This book made me cry, and I don't usually cry at sad things. The book is about a little girl's mother who is dying of cancer. The little girl is trying to believe that her mother will be okay.

There is one thing that I'm not crazy about in this book. The little girl never tells anyone about her problems. She just suffers. In this book, the author doesn't say how the mother dies. She just tells you the mother died. I would change that because I think readers want to know the truth (even though it's sad). I can tell you this book is worth reading.

Erika N. Mead, Grade 4
Newburgh, New York

Boonsville Bombers

by Alison C. Herzig

96 pages

Boonsville Bombers is a fiction book about a girl named Emma Lee who has a dream to be on her brother's baseball team. There's only one small problem: They don't want a girl on their baseball team. But Emma Lee has a plan. When they all go to a major league baseball game, she catches a ball that is hit by a famous ballplayer. If you ever saw the movie *Sandlot,* you will love this book. If you like to play baseball, you'll understand the book. Read this book and find out why Emma Lee gets to be on the baseball team.

**Richard Cipoletti, Grade 4
Dix Hills, New York**

Play Ball, Girls!

If you're like Emma Lee—a girl with an urge to play ball—then you may want to check out a local Little League team. Since 1974, this famous kids' league has opened up baseball to girls.

Letters From Rifka

by Karen Hesse

160 pages

This book tells the story of a girl named Rifka and her family. They were Jews who fled from Russia because they were not treated fairly.

Before Rifka was born, three of her brothers went to America. Rifka and her parents and two other brothers stayed in Russia. Later, the family tried to reunite in America. But Rifka had caught ringworm and was not allowed to travel. Her family left her with another family, whom she didn't know, so she could recover and join them later.

I really enjoyed this book because it was like reading someone's diary. I learned to appreciate the struggles that some people have gone through to be free and live in America. I would not want to be separated from my parents. Rifka's family really cared about each other. I think that is important for any family.

Did Rifka ever get to America? Read the book and find out.

**Callie Frank, Grade 5
West Hempstead, New York**

Eye Magic: Fantastic Optical Illusions—An Interactive Pop-up Book

by Sarah Hewetson

14 pages

ADVENTURE

ENVIRONMENT

MYSTERY

I read an amazing book called *Eye Magic: Fantastic Optical Illusions*. This book is worth reading because you can find all different tricks to do with your eyes! It's really cool! It made me feel like a professional magician. The book reminded me of a big magic store with lots and lots of tricks to do. If you read this book, you can be a magician, too!

Ashley Johnson, Grade 6
Actress

Shared Reading

There's nothing like a great book—except sharing it! Here's how:

1. **Read aloud.** Make it part of your family's daily routine.
2. **Start a book discussion group.** Ask a librarian or teacher to help.
3. **Read to someone who can't.** Check out *The Kid's Guide to Service Projects* by Barbara Lewis to find an audience who will appreciate a reader.

Ghosts in Fourth Grade

by Constance Hiser

80 pages

CHALLENGE/
COURAGE

DRAMA

THRILLS &
CHILLS

Ghosts in Fourth Grade is a thrilling book. It's about five kids who want to get even with a big bully. When they get a chance to scare him at the Hathaway house, something surprising happens. This book makes me feel good because the five kids stick up for themselves. I like how they planned it—they used a tape recorder, a pumpkin, and many other things. I recommend this book to anyone who has a bully.

David Beelman, Grade 5
St. Louis, Missouri

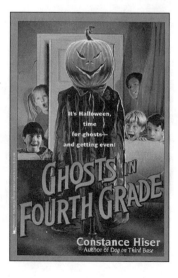

My Babysitter Has Fangs

by Ann Hodgman

128 pages

ADVENTURE

DRAMA

THRILLS & CHILLS

Last summer was a spooky one on Moose Island, Maine. Vincent the vampire was there, but Meg Swain and Jack Cornell were the only ones who knew it.

This summer, Vincent is back, only now his name is Victor Grable. Victor is dating Meg's next-door neighbor, Kelly Pitts. (Jack and Meg call her Pittsy.) Victor is using Pittsy to get to Meg, and Pittsy fell for Victor's trick.

Victor convinced Pittsy to kidnap Meg's little brother so that Meg and Jack would have to go rescue him from Victor. Then Victor would have them all in his hands!!!

If you want to find out what happens to Meg, Jack, Pittsy, and Meg's little brother, read this book. *My Babysitter Has Fangs* has pretty much of everything—action, suspense, romance, and drama. It was intense and kept me reading. There aren't many books that do that. This is why I think you should read *My Babysitter Has Fangs*.

**Nick Teach, Grade 7
New Berlin, Wisconsin**

Amazing Grace

by Mary Hoffman

24 pages

CHALLENGE/ COURAGE

DRAMA

This is an excellent book. It is about a girl named Grace. Grace and her class are doing a play called *Peter Pan*. Grace wants to be Peter Pan, but everyone says she is a girl and she is black. Will Grace be Peter Pan? I'm not going to spoil the story, so get a copy of *Amazing Grace*.

I like the story. It shows that it is not how you are outside, it is how you are inside that counts. You can do anything you put your heart and mind to.

**Lindsay Cardenas, Grade 4
Chula Vista, California**

Check It Out!

If you want to go with Grace on another, very different journey, check out *Boundless Grace*. In this sequel to *Amazing Grace*, Grace travels to Gambia in Africa, to visit her father—a man whom she barely remembers. While there, she explores the beauty of Gambian life and comes to realize that she has room in her heart for both of her far-apart parents.

Peach Boy

by William H. Hooks

48 pages

Peach Boy is one of the folktales most loved by Japanese children. This story has a little magic, scary demons, and a variety of friendly animals. The story begins with an old Japanese couple who are very poor and wish for a son. One day, while the old woman is washing out the clothes on a rock, a large peach comes floating down the stream. She takes home the large peach because she thinks it will feed them for a long time. Suddenly, they hear a voice from the peach, and a little boy appears! They name him Momototaro, which means, Peach Boy. When Peach Boy gets older, he decides to fight the Oni Monsters after they steal from their village. I won't tell you what happens when Peach Boy (Momototaro) meets the Oni Monsters, but I will tell you it's a very exciting part of the story! If you read this book, you will enjoy one of the Japanese children's favorite stories.

Erika Roehm, Grade 4
Syracuse, New York

Wild Weather: Tornadoes!

by Lorraine Jean Hopping

48 pages

I read this book called *Tornadoes!* It tells a lot about how tornadoes work and how much damage they can do. I couldn't do anything but read this book. I learned so much about tornadoes!

If you want to learn about a tornado, this is the perfect book for you. It tells how fast a tornado can go per hour. It has pictures of the damage it can do. One picture showed a house upside down, but everything was hooked together, like windows and doors and other stuff. I told my mom about this book. She read it. She loved it, too!

Monica Sawyers, Grade 4
Indianola, Iowa

Tornado Teaser

Tornadoes. Twisters. Cyclones. They're all the same—super powerful twisting windstorms. More precisely, they're rotating funnel clouds that extend *downward* from a mass of clouds. Did you know that tornadoes twirl counterclockwise in the Northern Hemisphere and clockwise in the Southern Hemisphere?

Bunnicula: A Rabbit Tale of Mystery

by James Howe

`100 pages`

Bunnicula is an awesome mystery-comedy book. It has seven main characters: Toby, Pete, Mr. and Mrs. Monroe, Chester, Harold, and Bunnicula. Toby and Pete are the brothers, Mr. and Mrs. Monroe are the parents, Chester is the cat, Harold is the dog, and Bunnicula is the bunny. Chester thinks Bunnicula is a vampire bunny because Bunnicula has fangs and an odd marking on his back. The Monroes found Bunnicula in a movie theater. The movie was about a vampire.

Soon the Monroes start finding white vegetables in the kitchen. The vegetables are dry with two holes in them. Chester knew that Bunnicula had sucked out all the juice in the vegetables. Chester got Harold to help him alert the Monroes that Bunnicula is a vampire bunny. Chester and Harold did all kinds of funny stuff to destroy Bunnicula.

My mom read *Bunnicula* and she loved it, too. That proves *Bunnicula* is for all ages!

**Sarah Holstein, Grade 5
St. Joseph, Michigan**

Trail of Apple Blossoms

by Irene Hunt

`64 pages`

Imagine saving the life of a trapped wolf and keeping it for a pet. In the book, *Trail of Apple Blossoms,* John Chapman did exactly that, because he did not believe in killing anything. This is an interesting book that tells the adventures of this brave, honest, and kind man. John Chapman is also known as "Johnny Appleseed." He didn't have much, except for his apple seeds, which he shared with others. He taught the settlers how to plant the seedlings, which grew into apple trees. John Chapman saved the lives of two children using different herbs and food. I am like John Chapman because I enjoy helping others, too. If people took lessons from John Chapman, our world would be a better place to live in.

**Laurie Sturm, Grade 4
East Brunswick,
New Jersey**

Check It Out!

Johnny Appleseed would be surprised to learn that farmers rarely grow apple trees from seeds today. Because apple farmers can't be sure what kind of apples will appear on trees grown from seeds, they usually buy their trees from nurseries. To learn how these trees are grown, check out *From Apple Seed to Applesauce* by Hannah Lyons Johnson.

Redwall

by Brian Jacques

352 pages

ADVENTURE

ANIMAL

HISTORY

This exciting book is about a group of mice and other creatures that live in an abbey called Redwall. They are attacked by a group of evil rats led by Cluny the Scourge. A young mouse, Matthias, must retrieve the mighty sword of the founder of the abbey to defeat Cluny and his horde.

This book reminds me of *Mrs. Frisby and the Rats of Nihm*. Redwall is just like this book, only it is in medieval times with badgers, squirrels, and moles. This time, there are no humans. Instead, there are evil creatures who are greedy for plunder and conquest.

Brian Jacques put small but incredibly detailed pictures at the beginning of each chapter. They give you a clue as to what the chapter will be about and will make you want to read on. If you are like me, you will often find yourself looking back at the picture during the chapter.

I definitely recommend this book to those who like adventure and nonstop action, with a dash of humor, in the medieval times.

Ryan Termeulen, Grade 5
Milford, Pennsylvania

Seasons of Splendour: Tales, Myths & Legends of India

by Madhur Jaffrey

128 pages

FANTASY & FOLKLORE

MULTICULTURAL

Seasons of Splendour is a collection of folktakes set in India. My favorite is "The Mango Tree," which describes the relationship between a brother and a sister, and between humans and all living things.

One day, the sister goes away and tells a servant to water her mango tree every day. She returns home when she hears that her brother is very ill and criticizes her servant for not watering the tree. The servant says that the sister is more concerned about the tree than about her brother. The sister shows how her brother and the tree share a common soul.

All of the stories are interesting because they are from another culture. I recommend this book to people who enjoy short stories and folktales.

Rishi Bhat, Grade 5
Actor

STAR REVIEW

Shoebag

by Mary James

ADVENTURE

ANIMAL

CHALLENGE/ COURAGE

144 pages

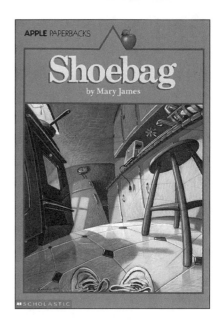

Shoebag is a wonderful book. It's about a cockroach who wishes to be bigger. One day, he wakes up as a small boy. How will he return to roachdom again? Read it and you'll find out.

I liked how Shoebag went through living with a human family instead of with roaches. This book made me feel eager to read. I recommend this book to someone who enjoys insects.

**Giuliana Morice, Grade 4
Glendale, Arizona**

Lift Every Voice and Sing

by James Weldon Johnson

HISTORY

MULTICULTURAL

36 pages

I like this book because I know its illustrator, Jan Spivey Gilchrist, and because my family modeled for it. In the book, there's even a special "thank you" to our family. We are thankful to Ms. Gilchrist for allowing us to be in her book.

I also like this book because it talks about the struggles of African Americans and their fight for freedom. "Lift Ev'ry Voice and Sing" is the African-American National Anthem. This song represents our freedom, and it's very exciting to be a part of it.

I recommend this book to all children because it is beautiful, and it tells the history of African Americans in a very special way.

**Crystal Cartwright, Grade 5
North Chicago, Illinois**

Lift Your Voice, Too

*Lift ev'ry voice and sing
Till earth and heaven ring,
ring with the harmonies of Liberty . . .*

Schoolchildren first lifted their voices to sing this dramatic song at a celebration of Abraham Lincoln's birthday in 1900. You can try to hit the high notes yourself if you have a piano and someone able to play the music at the end of the book.

The Great Barrier Reef: A Living Laboratory

by Rebecca L. Johnson

64 pages

Did you know that scientists consider the Great Barrier Reef in Australia a living laboratory? Well, they do! Scientists can find many answers—and a lot of new questions—just by studying it.

This book is filled with many interesting facts about coral reefs and the animals within them. For example, I never knew that there was a starfish named the crown-of-thorns. I learned it can destroy a whole reef!

In this book you get to sneak up on giant clams, figure out what the mysterious mound builders are, see how coral have offspring, and then learn what the offspring do. Enjoy!

Stefanie Nyman, Grade 5
Bloomington, Minnesota

Good Reef!

Coral reefs are growing all the time. Right now, coral covers about 80 million square miles of the globe. If you put the reefs all together, they would cover an area more than 25 times the size of the continental United States. The Great Barrier Reef is the world's largest reef, extending 1,200 miles across the Coral Sea, off

Nancy Drew: Bad Medicine

by Carolyn Keene

153 pages

Do you like spine-tingling mysteries that make your heart beat and your teeth chatter with fear? If you do, then you'll love *Bad Medicine*. When April Shaw, a young doctor, is visited by her father from St. Louis, he dies very mysteriously after an operation that was supposed to cure him! On top of that, April's fiancé is accused of murdering him!

It is mystery with just the right touch of horror here and there. But read carefully to pick up all the clues! Even if you are not able to solve the mystery, you won't be able to put this book down! Whether you like horror, mystery, or romance, this book has it all! I highly recommend it!

Helen Parson, Grade 5
Bronx, New York

Author! Author!

Although the Nancy Drew stories list Carolyn Keene as their author, she is not a real person. Neither is Franklin Dixon, "author" of the Hardy Boys. Both "authors" were creations of Edward Stratemeyer, who formed a syndicate to write series books. At first, Stratemeyer wrote the books himself. Now, his series are done by hired writers.

Nancy Drew: Secret in the Old Attic

by Carolyn Keene

177 pages

In *Secret in the Old Attic,* there is a detective named Nancy Drew who has to solve two mysteries. Nancy has to find the people who stole a dead man's music.

There is another mystery related to that one, and it is about someone who stole a unique silk-making process from another factory. To find out how she outwits the ruthless thieves, read this book! If you like mysteries, I'm sure you'll enjoy it.

Anne Novogunski, Grade 5 ·····
Mentor, Ohio

Rifles for Watie

by Harold Keith

352 pages

I just read this great book called *Rifles for Watie*. This book is about a boy named Jeff Bussey who can't wait to join the Union army during the Civil War. When Jeff is assigned as an infantry soldier, he must walk for miles and watch his friends die in battle. Then, when Jeff is sent as a spy behind enemy lines, he finds out that there is good and bad on both sides of the Civil War. My favorite part is when Jeff gets the Congressional Medal of Honor for what he does in battle. I recommend this book to people who like to read exciting, adventurous books about the Civil War.

Jon Bougher, Grade 5
Weare, New Hampshire

What's Watie?

Watie in this novel refers to Stand Watie, a Cherokee warrior who fought fearlessly for the Rebels (South) in south Kansas during the Civil War. But not all Cherokees in Kansas were "Watie Cherokees." Some fought against him on the Union (Northern) side.

Ralph's Secret Weapon

by Steven Kellogg

`48 pages`

Do you have an aunt who greets you with a banana-spinach cream cake and the news that you are spending your summer learning the bassoon? Well, in this book, Ralph's aunt does just that! His aunt's name is Georgiana, and boy is she strange. For example, after Ralph's first lesson, Georgiana decides he is so good that she signs him up for a snake-charming contest. Then Georgiana tells the navy that Ralph is the perfect one to catch a dreadful sea monster. The next day, Ralph boards the boat and . . .

If you want to find out what happens to the sea monster and what Ralph's secret weapon is, you'll have to read the book.

Catherine Munaco, Grade 3
Farmington Hills, Michigan

Ace, the Very Important Pig

by Dick King-Smith

`144 pages`

When Ace was born, farmer Tubs at once noticed that this piglet was different from the rest of the litter. Ace had a strange marking shaped like an ace of clubs on his left thigh (which is how he got his name). Not only does farmer Tubs notice that Ace is odd, but he also notices that Ace knows a lot more things than anyone expects.

Ace is too intelligent to go to market with the others, so Nanny, an old wise goat, and Clarence, a clever yellow-eyed cat, raise Ace like a family. Ace's popularity spreads all over England, and he becomes the most famous pig ever. Ace also becomes a house pig, just like a dog or a cat. At first, farmer Tubs is very shocked. Imagine if you came back from milking one day, and sitting in your comfy armchair is an enormous pig with an ace of clubs on his fanny watching the telly. How would you feel? It's pretty hard to believe, isn't it? Ace is a book about an important and civilized pig, and I recommend this book to anyone.

Annie Bodel, Grade 4
Highland Park, New Jersey

Check It Out!

The author of this book also wrote a book about another smart and talented pig. That book, *Babe, the Gallant Pig,* was later turned into the major motion picture *Babe.*

Kings, Gods and Spirits from African Mythology

by Jan Knappert

88 pages

This great book tells stories from Africa. It includes stories about spirits, magical animals, monsters, and legends! There are both colorful and black-and-white illustrations.

One story that I really enjoyed is "The Tortoise and the Hunter." The story is about a very good hunter. One day, he meets a hideous monster who demands half of each animal the hunter shoots! Every day the hunter comes home with only half of an animal. His wife becomes suspicious and goes hunting with her husband. When they arrive in the forest, the monster thinks the wife is an animal and demands half of her! Now they have to face him, for there is no turning back.

This book is very fun to read because everything about it has a very special moral. If you enjoy lessons, then you will enjoy this.

Brittany Crone, Grade 5
Cincinnati, Ohio

From the Mixed-up Files of Mrs. Basil E. Frankweiler

by E. L. Konigsburg

160 pages

Mrs. Basil E. Frankweiler is about what happens to twelve-year-old Claudia and nine-year-old Jamie. The story takes place in the Metropolitan Museum of Art in New York. The year is 1967.

Claudia wants to run away from home because her mom never pays any attention to her, but she always pays attention to her brothers Kevin, Steve, and Jamie. Claudia runs away with Jamie, since he has the most money ($24.43). The two set off to the Metropolitan Museum of Art, where they find a statue called *Angel.* Nobody knows who carved it, and Claudia and Jamie plan to find out.

This book is good for people who like mysteries set in the past. My favorite part is when Claudia washes the clothes in one load in the washer and dryer. When she takes them out, they're gray. I hope everybody enjoys this book as much as I did.

Liana Tallerico, Grade 4
El Cerrito, California

Lives of the Musicians: Good Times, Bad Times (And What the Neighbors Thought)

by Kathleen Krull

`96 pages`

A good book to read is *Lives of the Musicians* by Kathleen Krull.

This book gives interesting facts about famous musicians. The caricatures of each musician are funny to look at. I learned that you can probably make your own music if you try hard. Another thing I learned is that if your music is good, maybe you can be famous like Beethoven. I recommend this book to anyone who likes to laugh a lot. If you want to read this book and find out for yourself about great musicians, you can check it out in your library.

Brandon Dunn, Grade 5
Denton, Texas

Treasure Mountain

by Evelyn Sibley Lampman

`207 pages`

If you like Native American stories, then you will like *Treasure Mountain*. Hoxie and Irene are orphans in Chemawa. The reason they live there is that they have nowhere else to go. They find out they still have an Aunt Della in Nephlem. The story is about how three people become a family. I think people should read it because it shows how the Indians really feel about their beliefs.

Tosha Wilson, Grade 4
Madras, Oregon

Illustration Basics

Some tips for would-be illustrators:

1. **Learn to look.** Seeing how things really look is the heart of drawing well.
2. **Draw every day.** Most artists do.
3. **Experiment.** Try different ways of making lines, kinds of paint, collage, scratchboard, photography, print making.
4. **Examine books.** What do the illustrations add to the story? Try re-illustrating a book you love!

Invisible Bugs and Other Creepy Creatures That Live With You

by Susan S. Lang

96 pages

Did you know that raw termites taste like pineapple? Or that flies have five eyes? Did you know that fleas often bite in a Z shape? Or that every time you take a shower the bacteria on your body multiply? Disgusting, but true! We can't get away from bugs or bacteria. These fun facts and others are in this great book called *Invisible Bugs and Other Creepy Creatures That Live With You.* If you have the least interest in bugs, or want to freak out your friends, you should read this book.

Katrina Van Raay, Grade 5
Brooklyn, New York

Carry On, Mr. Bowditch

by Jean Lee Latham

256 pages

This is the story of a boy, Nathaniel Bowditch, who loved numbers. He had to leave school to help his father make barrels. When he was twelve, his father decided Nat would work better with his head than his hands and apprenticed him to a ship's chandler for nine years. Even though Nat couldn't go to school anymore, he never stopped learning, and he even taught himself Latin. An exciting part of the book is when Nat learned navigation and got to be captain of a ship. He wrote his own book of navigation, which is still used today. The best part of this story is that it is true. This book proves that even if you can't go to school, you can still learn a lot.

Gregory Gaff, Grade 5
Raleigh, North Carolina

Is It Totally True?

Actually, this book is not 100% true. It's what's known as "fictionalized biography." This means that the author based his or her book on the real facts but took the liberty of making up a few minor—or major—details. Why? Maybe to make a more entertaining story, or because there wasn't enough historical information to make the tale complete.

Rabbit Hill

by Robert Lawson

127 pages

Rabbit Hill is a very adventurous book. It is about a rabbit named Little Gorgie, the new folks, and Little Gorgie's other animal neighbors in the forest. When Gorgie overhears someone say new people are coming to live in the house, the whole forest is abuzz. Some animals are excited about people moving in, for they might grow a good, plentiful garden. But others, like Mamma Rabbit, are worried because they might bring dogs, cats, traps, guns, and even children!

I think Mamma Rabbit is pessimistic because she is always worrying, like when the new folks are coming. But I also think it is normal for her to worry, because she is Little Gorgie's mother, and mothers normally worry. This book taught me to be generous with my food, because some people don't have enough. I recommend this book for all ages. I quite enjoyed it!

Carrie Litty, Grade 5
Gales Ferry, Connecticut

To Kill a Mockingbird

by Harper Lee

288 pages

This is an age-old classic that shows the characters' true feelings. Jem Finch and his younger sister, Scout, spend fun-filled summers with their neighbor, Dill. When their father, Atticus, a respected lawyer in Maycomb County, Alabama, defends a black man, Jem and Scout must face the disapproval and jeering of their friends. This book is full of trust, love, hatred, humor, fear, kindness, and cruelty. This is my favorite book I ever, ever read, and I encourage others to read it also.

Maureen Olsen, Grade 6
Cheshire, Connecticut

A Movie to Match

If you loved the book, you'll love the movie, too. Too often this is not how it works out. But when the black-and-white film *To Kill a Mockingbird* came out in 1962, it got rave reviews and won two Academy Awards: Best Actor (Gregory Peck as Atticus) and Best Screenplay. See it for yourself on video.

Catwings

by Ursala K. LeGuin

64 pages

Catwings is a book about four cats that can fly! The cats' names are Thelma, James, Roger, and Harriet. Before they were born, their mother, Mrs. Jane Tabby, had a dream that her kittens would have wings, so they could fly away from the alley they lived in because it was filthy and they did not like it there one bit. When they get older, the four cats fly away so they can have a better life. But on the way, they have some adventures. I think you should read this book!!!

Leigh Urbschat, Grade 3 ••••••••••••••••••••
Longmeadow, Massachusetts

A Wrinkle in Time

by Madeleine L'Engle

224 pages

A Wrinkle in Time is my all-time favorite book. It's about Meg and her little brother, Charles Wallace. Their father was lost in a teserac. You'll have to read to find out what a teserac is. Charles Wallace meets three old ladies, and together Meg, Charles, Calvin, their friend, and the old ladies travel to different dimensions to save their father.

I recommend this book to anyone who is looking for a book with imagination. This book is very adventurous! After I read it, I could see it in my mind like a movie. This book is so real, you feel you're there. Again, I recommend this book strongly to anyone with an eye for adventure but who knows the true value of family and friends.

Lauren Erickson, Grade 5
Ojai, California

Believe It or Not

It was a dark and stormy night. Sound familiar? Ms. L'Engle opens *A Wrinkle in Time* with this famous line. It's famous because people joke about it being the classic way to start a novel. Even Snoopy's been known to begin more than a few unfinished novels with these words.

I Hate English!

by Ellen Levine

32 pages

I Hate English! makes me feel good.

Mei Mei is a Chinese girl. Mei Mei and her family have to move to America. She doesn't know why her family is going to America.

At the American school, Mei Mei didn't say anything. I knew she was very scared, because I came to America from Japan. My first day of school, I didn't say anything either.

If you read this book, you will know my feelings.

**Megumi Shimbo, Grade 3
Washington C. H., Ohio**

The Chronicles of Narnia

by C. S. Lewis

7 Books

The Chronicles of Narnia is one of the best series of books I've ever read! I plan to read it many more times.

The first book is *The Lion, the Witch and the Wardrobe.* Four English children must stay with their old uncle during World War II. Lucy discovers a doorway in a wardrobe that leads to Narnia, a wonderful world where plants and animals talk, and all the good people love the lion, Aslan. When Lucy returns, no one believes she's been anywhere but in the closet . . . until they all have to go to Narnia to rescue Edmund from the white witch who holds him by enchantment. This is how a terrific adventure begins. You'll hate to leave Narnia when *The Last Battle,* the final book in the series, is over.

**Ariana Richards,
Age 14
Actress**

STAR REVIEW

They're Classic

Beginning with the first in 1950, millions of copies of the seven books in C. S. (Clive Staples) Lewis's *Chronicles of Narnia* series have been sold around the world. They're considered "classics" in the world of children's literature because their popularity has withstood the test of time. As you can tell from these reviews, kids today continue to be entranced by the fantasy land of Narnia.

The Lion, the Witch and the Wardrobe

by C. S. Lewis

`160 pages`

This book is about four children, Peter, Susan, Edmund, and Lucy. One day, while playing hide-and-seek, they step into a magical wardrobe and find themselves in the once wonderful land of Narnia. Now it's ruled by a wicked witch. When the witch finds out they're in Narnia, she tries to capture them. Will Aslan, the mighty lion, rescue them, or will the witch find them and turn them into stone? If you want to find out what happens, read this exciting story yourself.

Stephanie Marple, Grade 5
Huben Heights, Ohio

The Magician's Nephew

by C. S. Lewis

`76 pages`

This book is exciting because Digory and Polly go into different worlds. They get to see things that people have not seen before, such as a witch, who almost kills them. Andrew, Digory's mean uncle, sent Polly away to another world. I wasn't sure she was going to be able to get back. They do some magic things, like putting wings on horses, and that never happens to me. And if I saw that, I would probably faint.

Digory, the main character, was very brave. I like people who are brave, because they go on exciting adventures, take risks, and take chances. Digory went to get Polly. He didn't know what was going to happen to him, but he knew he had to save his friend. Digory showed his courage when he went into different worlds. Polly didn't want to go. Digory talked to a lion. I would never do that. I would be too chicken. I would be scared the lion would bite my head off or something like that.

I think Polly is like me because if I had the choice of going to a different world or going home, I would probably go home. I would be too frightened. Polly and I are also very good listeners. We know what to do when we are asked.

Nicole Burge, Grade 4
Milwaukee, Wisconsin

The Silver Chair

by C. S. Lewis

208 pages

ADVENTURE

FANTASY & FOLKLORE

The Silver Chair is a tremendous book. It is about how a boy named Eustace (nicknamed Scrubb) and a girl named Jill Pole save a prince from the evil Emerald Witch's underground kingdom. This story is kind of strange, because in one part the Emerald Witch hypnotizes Jill and Scrubb. I enjoyed the illustrations in the beginning of each chapter. If you enjoy fantasy, you will be glad there are seven books all about fantasy in *The Chronicles of Narnia*.

Nicholas Sparks, Grade 5
London, Ohio

Striped Ice Cream

by Joan M. Lexau

96 pages

CHALLENGE/ COURAGE

FRIENDSHIP & FAMILY

Striped Ice Cream is a heartwarming story. It is about a girl named Becky whose birthday is coming up very soon. Becky is feeling very miserable. It is almost her birthday, but no one seems to care this year. She probably won't be able to have her favorite ice cream. Becky knows her family is too poor to buy presents, but what she doesn't know is why they have to be so mean to her. Her sisters and mother are making a dress and saying it is for her sister, Cecily. But on her birthday, she finds out her family does care about her. If you read the story, you will see why.

This book reminds me of the truths of life. It tells you about things that happen every day! I recommend this book to anyone who loves to read. It has only a little artwork, but the illustrations are beautiful.

Amy Chalice, Grade 4
Lapeer, Michigan

Pippi Longstocking

by Astrid Lindgren

158 pages

ADVENTURE

HUMOR

Pippi Longstocking is about a young girl who lives all by herself. People from the children's home try to take her away, but she is too strong and too tricky. No one can get her to the children's home, not even the police. Long ago Pippi sailed with her father, but one day a big storm came and he was never seen again. Pippi says he is king of the cannibals, and her mother is in heaven.

The book made me laugh a lot. Pippi reminds me of my friends— funny, tricky, and strong. More people should read *Pippi Longstocking*.

Melody Thompson, Grade 6
Orlando, Florida

Author! Author!

The inspiration for Swedish author Astrid Lindgren's award-winning Pippi Longstocking series came from her own daughter Karin. Recovering from pneumonia, she asked her mother to tell her a story about a girl named "Pippi Longstocking." Pippi Longstocking, and the more than one hundred books that followed, have been translated into many different languages so that children around the world may enjoy Pippi, too.

The Land of Gray Wolf

by Thomas Locker

32 pages

DRAMA

ENVIRONMENT

MULTICULTURAL

I just read a story about Indians that really made me think. It is about a young boy, Running Deer, who learned from his father, Gray Wolf, how to treat the land wisely and use only what is needed from nature. When settlers come to the Indians' land, what will happen? Will they fight or will they be able to work together? More importantly, what happens to the land? *The Land of Gray Wolf* is a great story and will answer these questions.

Jonathan Cohn, Grade 4
East Brunswick, New Jersey

The Call of the Wild

by Jack London

ADVENTURE

ANIMAL

DRAMA

I recommend a book called *The Call of the Wild*. It is jam-packed with adventure, excitement, and sadness. But don't worry, you won't cry. This book is for children who like to imagine things. It is so spectacular that you won't stop reading, even for a day at the ballpark!

After reading it, you will want to get a puppy to care for and love for the rest of its life. Check the book out at your local library and change the way you think about dogs!

**Timothy Grahn, Grade 6
Oak Forest, Illinois**

Shared Reading
There's nothing like a great book—except sharing it! Here's how:
1. **Read aloud.** Make it part of your family's daily routine.
2. **Start a book discussion group.** Ask a librarian or teacher to help.
3. **Read to someone who can't.** Check out *The Kid's Guide to Service Projects* by Barbara Lewis to find an audience who will appreciate a reader.

In the Year of the Boar and Jackie Robinson

by Betty Bao Lord

FRIENDSHIP & FAMILY

MULTICULTURAL

SPORTS

This is a fantastic book about an immigrant family who came to America from China. The family consists of a mother, a father, and a daughter named Shirley Temple Wong. The way she gets her name is hilarious!

Shirley doesn't speak much English and is having a hard time adjusting to the "American way." The twists and turns in this book will have you cheering Shirley on! This is a marvelous story, and I recommend it to anyone!

**Angie Wilkins, Grade 5
Frederick, Colorado**

Betsy and Tacy Go Over the Big Hill

by Maud Hart Lovelace

 ADVENTURE

DRAMA

`176 pages`

Betsy, Tacy, and Tib are three girls who live in the early 1900s in a small town in Minnesota. In this book, they become friends with someone who has come all the way from Syria to America to live a better life. They all decide they love America and wouldn't want to live anywhere else.

This is a great book because it's based on real people, only with changed names. I like it because it takes place in the old days, and I love to pretend I'm living back then. If you like their fun adventures, you'll be glad there is a whole series of books about these girls.

 STAR REVIEW

Mara Wilson, Grade 3 Actress

Extremely Weird Frogs

by Sarah Lovett

ENVIRONMENT

`48 pages`

This book is about many different kinds of frogs, from the tropical forests to the desert. This book also includes some poisonous frogs. I like this book because it lets you explore the world of frogs and toads.

There is a kind of extinct frog. When it laid its eggs, the female frog would swallow the eggs, and later in the year tiny frogs would hop out of the female's mouth. I thought that was pretty cool! To learn more about weird frogs, read this wild book.

**Zachary Guss, Grade 3
Palm Springs, California**

Check It Out!

If you found the frogs in Sarah Lovett's book to be wonderfully weird, you should be happy to know there are about a dozen more "Extremely Weird" books out there, all by Lovett. How about checking out *Extremely Weird Sea Creatures, Extremely Weird Micro Monsters,* or *Extremely Weird Primates*? Don't weird out!

The Three Little Javelinas

by Susan Lowell

ADVENTURE

ANIMAL

MULTICULTURAL

32 pages

I like *The Three Little Javelinas* because it is full of fun, adventure, and excitement. It is about a coyote blowing down the homes of the javelinas (*ha-ve-LEE-nas* means "wild pigs"), all except the last one. It is similar to *The Three Little Pigs,* but it takes place in a desert and has lots of interesting Spanish words like saguaro (*sa-WA-ro*), a kind of giant cactus.

If you don't read this book, the coyote will huff and he'll puff, and he'll blow your house in!

Alex Charfauros, Grade 4
Chula Vista, California

Attaboy, Sam!

by Lois Lowry

FRIENDSHIP & FAMILY

HUMOR

128 pages

If you like a funny and suspenseful story, then I think you will love *Attaboy, Sam!* This book is about a five-year-old boy named Sam. He wants to make his mom a birthday present. The birthday present is perfume that he makes himself. In order to do this, he goes around and collects all the smells his mother enjoys. For example, he knows his mother likes the smell of a baby. So one day, when his sister is babysitting, he collects a dirty diaper and puts it in a ziplock bag. Gag! My favorite part of the book is when the perfume exploded on his Dad, sister, and himself. I highly recommend this book because it is very, very, very funny.

Ryan Smith, Grade 5
Lansing, Michigan

Author! Author!

If you read all of the reviews of Lois Lowry's books on these pages, you'll notice that she covers a lot of territory as an author. Lowry, whose background includes journalism and photography, is comfortable writing hilarious books about the antics of Anastasia and Sam Krupnik, or novels like *A Summer to Die*, in which Meg deals with serious challenges, including her sister's death.

Author: Lois Lowry

The Giver

by Lois Lowry

208 pages

CHALLENGE/ COURAGE

DRAMA

Express Yourself

Like Alexie, who reviewed *The Giver,* have you ever been confused or disappointed by a book's ending, a twist in the plot, or a certain character? If so, you may want to write the author and express your thoughts—although you can also send a letter just to say how much you loved the book!

See the tips for writing to authors on page 30.

The Giver is a novel about a boy named Jonas who lives in a community where his life is run for him. He was given away at birth and then grew up as a "one," "two," "three," etc., until the age of twelve. Jonas was given different things at each age. When he was twelve, he was given a job. Jonas's job was a very important one. I won't tell you what it was, because the author builds up suspense for that. I can tell you that the Giver is his trainer. During Jonas's training, he realizes how horrible his community is, how his community would kill innocent people, even babies, just to follow the rules.

The book is well written, but the ending confused me. It does not fit the storyline of the rest of the book. This book was a Newbery-Medal Award winner. Mrs. Lowry's *Number the Stars* also won a Newbery Award, but is a much better book. Overall, *The Giver* was over-acclaimed.

**Alexie Atiya, Grade 5
Westchester, New York**

The Giver

by Lois Lowry

208 pages

CHALLENGE/ COURAGE

DRAMA

The Giver is about a young boy named Jonas who lives in a perfect world with no war or individuality. When children are twelve-years-old, they are given jobs they will carry out for the rest of their lives.

When Jonas is assigned the role of the next Receiver of Memory, he is amazed that he has been given the most honorable job in the community. But when he starts his training, he feels as though his childhood has been taken away. In the training you are given memories of what existed before the Committee of Elders (the group that controls the community) decided that they would eliminate individuality.

This book does not deal with everyday problems such as in Lowry's Anastasia series. I think that Jonas is one of the bravest characters I have read about. Anyone who enjoys unusual books will like this one.

**Kate Villard-Howe, Grade 5
Edgartown, Massachusetts**

Number the Stars

by Lois Lowry

ADVENTURE

CHALLENGE/ COURAGE

DRAMA

FRIENDSHIP & FAMILY

Number the Stars is about a Jewish girl named Ellen Rosen. She lives in Copenhagen and is best friends with a non-Jewish girl named Annemarie Johansen. The Nazis arrive in Copenhagen and look for Jews to take to the concentration camps. So Ellen moves in with the Johansen family. She pretends to be Annemarie's dead older sister. The girls have adventures and horrifying moments together.

In secret, Ellen and her family go on one compelling journey. Will Ellen and her family survive the trip? Annemarie also goes on a hard mission, but she is doing it to save her best friend's life. Will she make it? Find out in this terrific book!

I love *Number the Stars*. It is one of the best books I have ever read! *Number the Stars* is impossible to put down once you start reading it. This is just a suggestion: READ IT!

Ilana Messing, Grade 4
New York, New York

A Summer to Die

by Lois Lowry

CHALLENGE/ COURAGE

DRAMA

FRIENDSHIP & FAMILY

This book is about Meg and Molly, who are sisters; and they are very different. Molly is beautiful and popular, and Meg is plain. One day Molly comes down with leukemia. Meg goes to the hospital once to see Molly, but Molly is covered in wires and all her hair is gone, so it's hard to see her. One day, Molly closes her eyes and never opens them again. Meg and her parents are devastated.

Meg takes away her pain by teaching Will, her elderly friend, how to develop pictures. One day at a museum, her father shows Meg a picture of her that Will has taken. In the picture she sees a bit of Molly in her, and she knows that her time to be beautiful will come someday.

I recommend this book to anyone who would share the pain of the characters. I cried and used up almost two boxes of Kleenex. I learned some signs of leukemia and how people deal with it. I also learned that everyone's time to be beautiful will come, if not physically, then in the heart. I also learned that you don't need to compare yourself to anyone.

Emily Grenon, Grade 6
Somers, Connecticut

Letters From a Slave Girl: The Story of Harriet Jacobs

by Mary E. Lyons

`160 pages`

CHALLENGE/ COURAGE

FRIENDSHIP & FAMILY

HISTORY

Letters From a Slave Girl is a book that's worth one million dollars. It really touched my heart deeply and pulled me into the story. While reading it, I was Harriet Jacobs. It really made me understand what a good book is. I now know what life would have been like to have been a slave, to have had family die all my life, to be surrounded by hatred. Harriet Jacobs's life was sad but engrossing.

I highly recommend this book to anyone who has an interest in slavery. In *Letters From a Slave Girl,* you can understand slavery from the slaves' point of view. It is a challenging book, but not too challenging. It touched my heart and it will probably touch yours too.

**Lucy Allbaugh, Grade 4
Chelsea, Michigan**

Little House on Rocky Ridge

by Roger Lea MacBride

`368 pages`

ADVENTURE

ANIMAL

CHALLENGE/ COURAGE

HISTORY

Little House on Rocky Ridge is a good book about a little girl named Rose and her parents who go on a journey from South Dakota to Missouri in a covered wagon. This book made me feel like I was Rose, because I had to move once and had to make new friends.

I really liked the artwork because the illustrator used a pencil. I liked the book because I like to pretend that I am living in the olden days. This book is also about Laura Ingalls Wilder because Rose is her daughter. If you want to hear about what happens when she sees the tarantula, and when the new neighbors come over to help build the new barn, you will love this book.

Kayla Schlueter, Grade 4 ....
St. Cloud, Minnesota

The Little Island

by Golden MacDonald

48 pages

ANIMAL

ENVIRONMENT

The Little Island is a cool book. I like *The Little Island* because I love islands. I've been to an island. I took my cat, who explored the island the same way the cat in the book does. The book is neat because it explains that an island is not just a piece of floating land, it stands on the earth. I think you would like *The Little Island* because it tells a lot about islands.

**Caitlin Gerber, Grade 3
New Gloucester, Maine**

Author! Author!

The name Golden MacDonald might not be familiar to you, but her work probably is. Ask your parents if the words, "In the great green room..." ring a bell! This book was actually written by Margaret Wise Brown, writing under a pseudonym. She is best known for *Goodnight Moon* and *The Runaway Bunny,* two classics for younger children.

Baby

by Patricia MacLachlan

132 pages

**CHALLENGE/
COURAGE**

**FRIENDSHIP
& FAMILY**

POETRY

I love babies, but I am the baby in my family, so I'll never get a baby sister or brother. My parents gave me the book *Baby* by Patricia MacLachlan. It is a sad book about love and poetry that takes some thinking about. I love the grandmother character, Byrd.

My mom and I took turns reading this book out loud. She reads one page, then I read one page. *Baby* reminded my family to play the game "rock, paper, scissors" and to eat spice cake.

Patricia MacLachlan wrote this book for all ages. It will make you cry and laugh. Why don't you check it out?

**Eva Schnurr, Grade 4
Amherst, Massachusetts**

Author! Author!

Patricia MacLachlan was an only child, so she made up brothers and sisters. "That's how I learned to play out themes, to develop characters, to hear other voices," she says. "When I drive along in my car, I have conversations with my characters. People think I'm singing along with the radio."

**Author:
Patricia
MacLachlan**

Sarah, Plain and Tall

by Patricia MacLachlan

`64 pages`

ADVENTURE

CHALLENGE/ COURAGE

FRIENDSHIP & FAMILY

HISTORY

Sarah, Plain and Tall takes place on the western prairies of the United States. Sarah, Jacob, Anna, and Caleb are the main characters. They are a family of three until Sarah, from Maine, comes into their lives. This book has deep feelings of love, fear, and hope.

The story starts with Anna telling Caleb, her brother, about their mother. The big news of the day is when Jacob, their papa, informs them that he has placed an ad in the newspaper for a wife and a mother. After a little time passes, Sarah answers the ad and comes to visit.

The Witting family shares their prairie life with Sarah. Sarah learns about farming, the weather, sheep, and driving the wagon. In return, Sarah tells them about the sea, shells, painting, and the sand dunes. Will Sarah stay with the family, or will she go back to Maine?

I enjoyed the book because I learned more about the earlier days in America. It was interesting to see how a young girl lived then. I think Anna had more work to do than I do. I recommend this book to others and would enjoy reading other books by this author.

**Jessica Sheets, Grade 5
Jackson, Mississippi**

Back Home

by Michelle Magorian

`384 pages`

CHALLENGE/ COURAGE

HISTORY

MULTICULTURAL

*A*n English girl named Virginia (Rusty, for short) returns to her true home in England after being evacuated to America for five years during World War II. Her mother wants Rusty to be a proper English girl, but Rusty is a true American at heart. She even has an American accent.

Back Home is a great book because it shows a girl who has to adjust to the English way of life after living in America for five years. She was used to peanut butter and jelly and lots of milk each day; now she has to eat liverwurst and get used to rationed food.

Rusty has to go to a boarding school in England. Like me, she has to wear a uniform. She hates it there because she has to wear a uniform.

Will Rusty manage to adapt to the English way of life? Find out in *Back Home*.

**Sarika Govind, Grade 5
Cincinnati, Ohio**

Good Night, Mr. Tom

by Michelle Magorian

336 pages

CHALLENGE/
COURAGE

FRIENDSHIP
& FAMILY

HISTORY

Good Night, Mr. Tom takes place in London during World War II. Willie Beeck is a timid boy who is the abused child of a single mother. He has to be evacuated to the English countryside, where he meets a loving, caring man named Mr. Tom. Gradually, he learns to love a world he never knew existed and to forget the despair of his past. After a long period of time, Willie has to return to his mother. After weeks without word from Willie, Tom sets out for London to search for the boy he has come to love as his own son.

I think this story has a lot to do with the way children are being abused in everyday life. It is recommended to fifth and sixth graders.

**Jennifer Lappas, Grade 6
Bronx, New York**

Check It Out!

Wars don't affect only the soldiers who fight. Here reviewers tell us about two books by Michelle Magorian exploring the huge changes World War II brought to the lives of two English school kids. Look for *Not a Swan,* another book by Magorian set in the same period.

Scared Stiff

by Jahnna N. Malcolm

128 pages

ADVENTURE

THRILLS &
CHILLS

A seventh grade girl named Kelly lives smack in the middle of a cemetery. Her parents are morticians and work on dead people. One night Kelly's parents are out to a movie, and her brother is having a friend spend the night. The three kids sneak into Kelly and Chance's dad's laboratory. They find a corpse who comes to life. The corpse locks them in and goes out to murder the people who put him in jail. Can they stop him?

I highly recommend this book. It's a book my class enjoyed, and you will too! Trust me, *Scared Stiff* is a story you'll never forget!

Megan Megli, Grade 5 · · · · · · · · · · · ·
Olathe, Kansas

The Slime That Ate Sweet Valley

by Jahnna N. Malcolm

144 pages

The Slime That Ate Sweet Valley is about a girl named Maddy who just recently moved to a desert town called Crestview Estates; a boy named Keegan, who also just moved there; and the smart one in the group, Einstein, who has lived in Crestview Estates for a while. They all have to battle toxic green and purple slime. I like the part at the end when Maddy discovers what to use to fight the slime. It is an exciting story, and it reminds me of my uncle who used to live in the desert.

I think other people should read it, because the book is always full of suspense. There is only one way to execute this grotesque monster, but you'll have to read it for yourself to find out.

Jason Pilchuk, Grade 4
Sterling, Virginia

My Dad Lives in a Downtown Hotel

by Peggy Mann

92 pages

This book made me feel very sad because a boy named Joel has a very big problem with his parents. They want to get divorced.

I did not exactly like the main character, Joel. He is too gullible. He thinks that everything is his fault, and it really gets annoying. There are a few pictures in this book, but I did not really enjoy them since they are not in color, and I could not understand them.

If I had a choice to change the book a bit, I would probably make Joel a little bit younger. It would be more interesting. I did not really learn anything from this book, but I started thinking about what would happen if my parents got divorced. I would be very angry, but I know it will never happen. I did learn to tell my parents my true feelings and not to keep any secrets from them.

This book reminded me of another book that I have read called *Matilda*. It was about a girl whose parents were very mean to her. At the end of the book, Matilda ends up with a teacher who takes care of her.

Nathalie Greenstone, Grade 5
St. Laurent, Province of Quebec, Canada

Breaking Up Is Hard to Do

In *My Dad Lives in a Downtown Hotel,* Joel has difficulty dealing with his parents' divorce. These problems are probably all too familiar to friends of yours, or to you personally. About a million American children face the divorce of their parents every year.

The Computer That Ate My Brother

by Dean Marney

128 pages

The Computer That Ate My Brother is a very good book. It is about a boy named Harry Sith who wanted a drum set for his birthday, but instead he got a computer. The first thing Harry realized about his computer was that it was not normal. It cried, wrote messages, and flashed the living room lights off and on when it wanted attention. The second thing Harry realized about his computer was its ability to read his mind. I like this book because I've never experienced such a crazy computer. This book made me feel a bit happy that I've never owned a computer, because I would never want to experience what happened to Harry. I recommend this book, or any other books by Dean Marney, because they are very interesting.

**Melissa Rendos, Grade 6
Bronx, New York**

The Jack-O'-Lantern That Ate My Brother

by Dean Marney

96 pages

Do you have a brother? Did you ever wish he would disappear? That's exactly what happened to Elizabeth in this exciting book.

One Halloween night Elizabeth goes trick-or-treating. Her brother, Booker, has to tag along. Many scary, weird, and spooky things happen to them. When they get to a strange house, a witch comes out and offers Booker candy from a huge jack-o'-lantern. He touches the jack-o'-lantern and disappears into it! The rest of the story describes Elizabeth's haunted journey trying to find her brother.

The book made me interested in finding out what happened. I liked the book because it made me laugh. One part that made me really laugh was when Elizabeth says, "This totally ugly woman came by. I mean ugly. She had a nose you could hang clothes on."

The characters of Elizabeth and Booker reminded me of my sister Katie and me. We fight a lot and don't get along very well. But even though we don't get along, we still love each other. If she ever got lost like Booker did, I would try everything to find her, too.

**Karen Merrill, Grade 3
Depew, New York**

California Girls
(Baby-sitters Club Super Special Series #5)

by Ann M. Martin

240 pages

FRIENDSHIP & FAMILY

MYSTERY

This book is about seven girls who formed a baby-sitters club. The baby-sitters club wins the lottery, and with the money, they go on a trip to California to visit Dawn Schafer's dad and her brother, Jeff. Stacey McGill is taking surfing lessons with these other teenagers who drive like maniacs, and she almost gets killed once. Mallory Pike gets a whole makeover, and she's not allowed to wear makeup yet!

I recommend this book to girls who like baby-sitting and adventures! When I read this book it feels like I'm really there! It's a really good book.

Allison Walden, Grade 3
Mechanicsburg, Pennsylvania

Author! Author!

Ann M. Martin is usually working on three books at a time: one for the *Baby-sitters Club* series, one for the *Baby-sitters Little Sisters* series, and one nonseries book. And she does all that writing with a fountain pen, not a computer. No wonder she's up at 5:30 every workday morning!

Author: Ann M. Martin

Jessi's Secret Language
(Baby-sitters Club #16)

by Ann M. Martin

176 pages

FRIENDSHIP & FAMILY

MYSTERY

I like this book because it tells us that all kids are the same inside, but different on the outside. It shows a special relationship between Matt (a handicapped kid) and Jessi. It shows that everyone can learn a secret language. I think more people should care about handicapped kids like Jessi. You'll have to read the book to find out what Jessi does and all about the secret language.

Caddie Nesset, Grade 4
St. Michael, Minnesota

Karen's Toothache
(Baby-sitters Little Sister Series #43)

by Ann M. Martin

112 pages

Karen has a bad toothache, but she does not want to go to the dentist. When it is time to go, she hides in a tree. Her mother gets worried and is about to call the police, so Karen climbs down.

I thought this book was funny, especially when Karen thought she was going to die at the dentist's office. It reminded me of my little sister, because she always hides when we go to the dentist. I would recommend this book to anyone who ever had a toothache!

**Lauren Huber, Grade 4
Leesburg, Virginia**

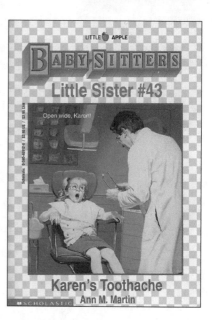

Kristy and the Missing Child
(Baby-sitters Club Mystery Series #4)

by Ann M. Martin

160 pages

It all starts when eight-year-old Jake Kuhn is reported missing. His parents are divorced, and Mrs. Kuhn thinks that Mr. Kuhn could have taken him. He was last seen by Kristy, Thomas, and Bart Taylor as they were coming home from a softball game. But Jake never returns home. His mother searches all over the town. She calls everybody she knows and still can't find him. She even gets the police to look for clues to help find him. They only find one clue—a letter from a woman to Jake's father. Kristy and Bart help to try to find him. Where is he? You'll have to read the book to find out.

**Suzanne Apicos, Grade 4
Staten Island, New York**

Mary Anne and the Secret in the Attic
(Baby-sitters Club Mystery Series #5)

by Ann M. Martin

160 pages

FRIENDSHIP & FAMILY

MYSTERY

I really liked *Mary Anne and the Secret in the Attic*. Mary Anne is the main character. When Mary Anne went up in the attic, she found a box. In the box there were letters. One letter she read was about her mother. The second was about her grandparents. The last one was about her living with her grandparents. Were her grandparents her real guardians? That's what Mary Anne wonders. Me, too: I just couldn't wait until I finished this book. It is that great! There is always excitement. There are no pictures in this book, but I didn't mind. Ann M. Martin included good descriptions, so I just pictured things in my head.

Author:
Ann M. Martin

Tara Bussey, Grade 4
East Brunswick, New Jersey

Knots on a Counting Rope

by Bill Martin, Jr., and John Archambault

32 pages

ANIMAL

CHALLENGE/ COURAGE

FRIENDSHIP & FAMILY

MULTICULTURAL

Do you like stories about people with problems? I do, and that's why *Knots on a Counting Rope* is a favorite book of mine. It is about Boy-Strength-of-Blue-Horses, a Native American boy who is blind but has the love and support of his family and friends. I am an Alaskan native, and I love nature just like Boy-Strength-of-Blue-Horses. I could read this book over and over and still want to read it again.

Katrina Stone, Grade 6
Chiniak, Alaska

Check It Out!

A story can make cold facts come alive and become more real. If you find *Knots on a Counting Rope* a good way to explore Native American culture, try *Amee-Nah: Zuni Boy Runs the Race of His Life* by Kenneth Thomasma, or *The Boy Who Made Dragonfly: A Zuni Myth* retold by Tony Hillerman.

Daniel's Story

by Carol Matas

144 pages

Daniel's Story by Carol Matas is an exciting story about Daniel and his life as a Jew.

Daniel's town is being invaded by Nazis during World War II. I like Daniel because he is bold, daring, and brave, even when the Holocaust has started and he is put in a concentration camp.

I think everyone should read this book because it will teach you to be thankful for everything you have.

**Stephanie Lauer, Grade 4
Appleton, Wisconsin**

The Lost Locket

by Carol Matas

80 pages

I really hate to lose anything. It is even worse when a friend finds it and knows it's yours but won't give it back to you. That is what *The Lost Locket* is about.

Roz loses her grandma's gold locket, and she can't get it back from Curtis, the bully who found it. Roz is afraid to tell her mother. Sometimes I feel like that.

This book, *The Lost Locket*, makes me feel good and tells me how important it is to go to your parents when you have a problem. I liked the sketches that were in this book too. I hope you read this book.

**Jennifer Reddick, Grade 4
Howick, Province of Quebec, Canada**

All the Days of Her Life

by Lurlene McDaniel

160 pages

CHALLENGE/ COURAGE

DRAMA

Have you ever wondered what it would be like to experience a life-or-death situation? In *All the Days of Her Life,* Lacey Duval found herself in just that position.

Lacey is a teenage girl who has diabetes. When Lacey returns to high school, she thinks that fitting in with the rest of the crowd means losing weight. So she starts fiddling with her insulin dosage and sometimes skips meals altogether. For a diabetic, this means trouble.

From this particular story, I learned that facing the truth about your problems is a lot better than taking the consequences when you ignore them.

This book would probably appeal to girls more than boys, although I would recommend it to all people who are trying to change themselves to fit in. Here's some advice: It's better just to be yourself!

Elizabeth Whiteley, Grade 6
Somers, Connecticut

Author! Author!

When Lurlene McDaniel's son nearly died from juvenile diabetes, she saw firsthand the strength and courage a child can possess. The experience changed her life—and her writing. As McDaniel says, "No one can control what life dishes out. What you can control is how you respond to it."

Baby Alicia Is Dying

by Lurlene McDaniel

192 pages

CHALLENGE/ COURAGE

DRAMA

FRIENDSHIP & FAMILY

Desi is a volunteer at the Childcare House, where they keep HIV-positive kids. Desi's favorite child is Alicia. Desi tries to spend as much time as she can with her. If you're wondering why the kids are HIV positive, it's because their mothers shared needles to do drugs. Desi is very worried about what's going to happen to the babies, especially Alicia.

Desi finds out that Alicia's mother wants to see her daughter. When the day comes, Desi does everything to make Alicia look beautiful. Desi follows Alicia and her mother, because she doesn't want anything to happen to baby Alicia. Then she asks herself, "Why am I doing this?" So she goes home. A few days later, Alicia gets really sick. Do you think Alicia will die? To find out, read this depressing, but hopeful, book.

After reading *Baby Alicia Is Dying,* I now understand more about AIDS and HIV-positive children and adults.

Amanda Gerber, Grade 5
St. Joseph, Michigan

I Want to Live

by Lurlene McDaniel

128 pages

CHALLENGE/
COURAGE

DRAMA

FRIENDSHIP
& FAMILY

I just read this really emotional book called *I Want to Live*. It was about this girl named Dawn who has leukemia but has been in remission for almost a year. Then, suddenly, she has a relapse, and her brother, Rob, has to give her more bone marrow.

Dawn has now been in the hospital for a while and is starting to get better. She gets to leave the hospital for one evening and goes out to dinner with her family. Things are really looking good.

Suddenly, everything takes a turn for the worse. What will happen to Dawn? Will she die like her friend Sandy? To find out, read this powerful story.

Danae Kovac, Grade 5
St. Joseph, Michigan

Six Months to Live

by Lurlene McDaniel

144 pages

CHALLENGE/
COURAGE

DRAMA

FRIENDSHIP
& FAMILY

This book is kind of happy and kind of sad. It is fiction, but it taught me a lot about cancer. The main characters are Dawn and Sandy. I felt happy for Dawn, but sad for Sandy. The book is about two girls who have cancer, and when they share a hospital room, they become great friends. While they are in the hospital, a doctor recommends they go to a camp where there are other kids with cancer. They have a great time at camp. I liked Dawn because she always had hope. I liked Sandy because she always was nice. There are no pictures in this book, but you almost get visions of what is happening. This book is like another book I read by Lurlene McDaniel, called *Mourning Song*. They are both about people in the hospital, except *Mourning Song* is about a girl with a brain tumor who wants to go to Florida (to see the beach). This book really made me think about how lucky I am not to have any disease or problem.

Kristen Consolo, Grade 6
Bay Village, Ohio

So Much to Live For

by Lurlene McDaniel

CHALLENGE/
COURAGE

DRAMA

FRIENDSHIP
& FAMILY

160 pages

So Much to Live For is a really good book. It's about a girl named Dawn who has leukemia. Dawn is doing really well and she has been in remission for almost three years. Dawn decides she would like to go to a cancer camp to be a counselor.

Dawn has fun—until Marlee comes. Marlee is a very bratty girl who doesn't have friends. Besides trying to take over Dawn's bed, Marlee is mean to the other girls. Dawn tries to open up to Marlee by talking to her, but she clams up and walks away. People try to help her, but she screams at them.

Then Marlee gets very sick and wants Dawn to come and see her. What will Dawn do? Read this book and see.

Megan Green, Grade 5
St. Joseph, Michigan

Too Young to Die

by Lurlene McDaniel

CHALLENGE/
COURAGE

DRAMA

FRIENDSHIP
& FAMILY

176 pages

Melissa Austin lives in Tampa, Florida, and goes to Lincoln High. Her best friend, Jory Delaney, is from a wealthy family, and she likes Melissa's older brother, Michael. Melissa wants to be on the Brain Bowl team and win a National Merit Scholarship. But when she is stricken with leukemia (blood cancer), she doesn't know if she will survive.

She goes to the hospital and meets Ricter Davis, who has bone cancer and a prosthetic limb. Ricter gives her hope of overcoming her disease, since he will soon be released from the hospital. She also meets a girl named Rachel Dove, who is the cutest little girl she has ever seen.

When Melissa gets out of the hospital, Jory buys her a wig for Christmas. It is cut short with black hair, and Melissa really likes it since she has lost her hair due to the chemotherapy. The following week, when she returns to the hospital for blood work, she discovers that Rachel died the night before, which makes her very sad. It also makes her appreciate the fact that she is still alive.

Be sure to read this touching and inspirational novel. I enjoyed it a lot, and I'm sure you also will.

Sarah Slocomb, Grade 6
Beach, North Dakota

Snow Treasure

by Marie McSwigan

`160 pages`

I loved *Snow Treasure*. I give it two thumbs-up. It was exciting from start to finish.

The book takes place in 1940, during World War II, in a small village in Norway. The German army has just occupied the village and is after the village's gold. Four kids have to get past the soldiers, sledding down a mountain holding gold in lunch bags without being caught.

Besides being exciting, S*now Treasure* is also funny. I learned about another country in another time. I've read *Snow Treasure* a lot of times and each time I liked the book just as much as the time before.

Max Pomeranc, Grade 4 ....
Actor

STAR REVIEW

Moby-Dick

by Herman Melville, adapted by Patricia Daniels

`624 pages`

I recommend this book because of the adventure and excitement. It's about a sea captain who chases a whale named Moby Dick. This book reminds me of times when my dad and I go sailing on his sailboat. We see whales all the time, and I do believe they are as strong as the book shows. I have always wanted to go sailing like Captain Ahab, even though I didn't like him very much because he was crazy.

Joel Dicola, Grade 6
Seattle, Washington

A Whale of a Tale

Moby-Dick is the great fisherman's tale—"the one that got away"—in American literature. The great white whale escapes his hunters by turning on them. Read this adaptation of the classic novel to find out what happens next. *Moby-Dick* is also a good way to learn about whaling, a dangerous and romantic occupation 150 years ago.

Long Meg

by Rosemary Minard

64 pages

Take a trip into the past with *Long Meg*. It is about a tall girl who works in the King's Inn and wants to do more than scrub floors and serve dinners. She wants adventure. One day, she finally gets her wish. Dressed as a swordsman, she goes to France as a soldier planning a sneak attack against the French. All the soldiers are sick and she's left to defend everyone, even though she has a broken leg. I liked this book because it taught me that if you stick to something, it just might happen.

**Karli Tucker, Grade 4
East Brunswick, New Jersey**

Illustration Basics

Some tips for would-be illustrators:

1. **Learn to look.** Seeing how things really look is the heart of drawing well.
2. **Draw every day.** Most artists do.
3. **Experiment.** Try different ways of making lines, kinds of paint, collage, scratchboard, photography, print making.
4. **Examine books.** What do the illustrations add to the story? Try re-illustrating a book you love!

Baseball Saved Us

by Ken Mochizuki

32 pages

If you want to read a really exciting book about baseball, try *Baseball Saved Us*. Even if you hate baseball, you'll like this book.

The story takes place in a Japanese-American internment camp during World War II. While in the camp, one father builds a baseball field to fight boredom. His son, Shorty, succeeds at baseball because he puts his anger into his hitting and turns his hatred of prejudice into something good.

The illustrations almost tell the story without words. The brown colors represent not only the desert setting but also the boy's unhappiness. This is a good book for people who like baseball, suspense, history, or books with strong feelings.

**Mrs. Watson's Class, Grade 5
Chapel Hill, North Carolina**

The Flying Tortoise

retold by Tololwa M. Mollel

ANIMAL

FANTASY & FOLKLORE

MULTICULTURAL

32 pages

The Flying Tortoise is a very funny tale of the Igbo people of southeastern Nigeria. I like the main character, Mbeku the tortoise, because he is always tricking the other animals into doing something for him. One example is when he tricked the birds into giving him feathers so that he could fly.

The artwork in this book is well done. It is colorful and humorous; it helps you see the story happen.

This story teaches a good lesson. The lesson is that it might be fun to play tricks on other people, but their feelings might get hurt and they won't trust you again. I think that there is an important lesson in this book for everybody.

**David Schmerler, Grade 5
Cincinnati, Ohio**

Anne of Green Gables

by L. M. Montgomery

ADVENTURE

FRIENDSHIP & FAMILY

HUMOR

108 pages

Anne of Green Gables is about an orphan girl who is adopted by a brother and sister, Matthew and Marilla Cuthbert. I like Anne because she has a great imagination and is always getting herself into awkward situations. One of the relationships Anne has in the book is with a boy named Gilbert. She hates him because he calls her "carrot head." Anne hates having red hair.

When I was finished reading this book, I continued thinking about what it would have been like if I had lived on Prince Edward Island in the 1800s.

If you think you would like reading about an 11–15-year-old girl who lived in the 1800s, this book is exactly right for you.

**• • • • Allison B. Greenberg, Grade 5
Cincinnati, Ohio**

> ## Hold That Thought!
> Do you ever make notes to yourself in a journal or diary? One quiet spring day, L. M. (Lucy Maud) Montgomery was glancing through an old notebook of hers and saw this: "Elderly couple apply to orphan asylum for a boy. By mistake a girl is sent." From that little idea, jotted down many years before, was born the irrepressible Anne of Green Gables.

Who Let Girls in the Boys' Locker Room?

by Elaine Moore

144 pages

Can boys at Jefferson Junior High ever get used to girls on the boys' basketball team? Well, the only way you can find out is by reading, *Who Let Girls in the Boys' Locker Room?*.

This book is about fifth-grade girls going into sixth grade junior high. They want to join the girls' basketball team, but they have to combine both girls' and boys' basketball teams. Most of the girls make the team, except for one. Finally, she does get accepted. You'll have to read the rest to find out what happens. I don't want to spoil the end for you.

It is a great story for people who love basketball, like me. The games in the book are super exciting. I would definitely read it again.

Mia Joanne Dinnan, Grade 6
Lapper, Michigan

Crystal

by Walter Dean Myers

208 pages

In my opinion, *Crystal* is one of the best children's novels of all time. It's by African-American author Walter Dean Myers. Crystal is a sweet girl who has one of those beautiful faces you just can't stop staring at. She is offered a contract to be a model for a company. She takes up the offer. Will Crystal still be that sweet girl everybody likes? You wouldn't want me to spoil the book for you, would you?

Top Five Ways to Find a Good Book

5. Read book review.
4. Read over someone's shoulder. (But don't let him or her catch you!)
3. Check out the award winners at the library or bookstore.
2. Ask a friend, parent, librarian, or teacher.
1. Read this book!

I like this book because I've always wanted to know what it's like being a model with all of those cameras looking at you. I also like this book because it has a very important moral: It's not the outside, it's the inside that counts.

Keewa Nurullah, Grade 6
Chicago, Illinois

131

Journey to Jo'burg: A South African Story

by Beverly Naidoo

96 pages

ADVENTURE

CHALLENGE/ COURAGE

FRIENDSHIP & FAMILY

MULTICULTURAL

Journey to Jo'burg is about two children who live in a small village in South Africa with their auntie and grandmother. Their baby sister becomes ill, and they must travel to the big city of Johannesburg to find their mother. On the way, they have lots of adventures.

I really like this book. It's about my African heritage, and history is my best subject. It reminds me of what happened in the South in our own country in the 1950s and 1960s. I think everyone should read this gripping book to find out about the racial trouble that is going on even now in South Africa.

**Tenicka T. Hatchett, Grade 4
Milwaukee, Wisconsin**

A World Turning

A lot has changed in South Africa since the period described in Beverly Naidoo's novel. Nelson Mandela is now president. Africans can vote, and apartheid—laws of segregation—has been abolished. There are still huge problems, but the world rejoices in the changes the last decade has brought.

Shiloh

by Phyllis Reynolds Naylor

144 pages

ANIMAL

FRIENDSHIP & FAMILY

Shiloh is the best book I've ever read. It's about a mean man named Judd Travers who buys dogs and then mistreats them. Then one day, a boy named Marty finds one of Judd's dogs and names him Shiloh after the Shiloh Schoolhouse. Marty's dad makes him take Shiloh back to where he found him, but Shiloh comes back. Marty keeps him a secret. Soon everybody finds out, except Judd.

I liked Marty because whenever the author made his heart go thumpity-thump, you can feel your heart doing the same thing.

Shiloh reminded me of the beagle pup I used to have. And Marty reminded me of how I treated him. If you love dog stories, you'll surely love this book.

**Dustin Kubasek, Grade 4
Ashland, Ohio**

Check It Out!

Animals can bring out the best and worst in our behavior, and writers have used them to show the whole range of human potential. If you like *Shiloh,* check out these canine greats of literature: *The Call of the Wild* by Jack London and *Lassie Come Home* by Eric Knight. Fetch them from your local library!

The Borrowers

by Mary Norton

180 pages

The Borrowers is a book about three little people who are the size of your fingernail. These little people borrow things from human beings like lace, blotting paper, doll chairs, tables, and other accessories. This particular family lives under the floor beneath the stove. Their names are Pod, Homily, and Arrietty Borrowing. Arrietty wanders off and starts playing. Then she notices somebody's watching her. If you want to find out what happens after she's seen, then read *The Borrowers*.

The author is Mary Norton; the illustrators are Beth and Joe Krush. It is very exciting! I hope you like it! Bye!

Lauren Holbrook, Grade 6
Crested Butte, Colorado

Black Star, Bright Dawn

by Scott O'Dell

144 pages

Do you like to read a good adventure book? If you do, you will love *Black Star, Bright Dawn*, by Scott O'Dell. This book is about a young Eskimo girl named Bright Dawn, who sets off on the Iditarod, a scary dogsled race over trails covered with ice and snow. Bright Dawn and her dog, Black Star, run into problem after problem on this thousand-mile race from Anchorage to Nome, Alaska. It's an exciting book to read, and it makes you feel good!

.......**Janna Hutchins,**
Grade 4
Lake Forest, Illinois

Island of the Blue Dolphins

by Scott O'Dell

192 pages

In the middle of the Pacific Ocean there lies an island that is shaped like a great fish. This island is called the Island of the Blue Dolphins. Karana lives on the Island of the Blue Dolphins with her tribe, the Ghabs-at. Her father, Chief Chowing, is the ruler of the tribe. One day a large ship comes into sight. All of the village people are curious about why the ship is here. The people are there for pelts. Eventually, there is a war. Karana's father and most of the hunters die. The pelt takers leave, and the tribe goes by ship to another island. Karana's brother is left behind; she dives off the ship to be with her brother on the island. Her brother tries to kill the pack of wild dogs. He dies in the process, and she is now alone on the island. You have to read the book to find out how she survives.

Author! Author!

The setting for *Island of the Blue Dolphins* is very much like Terminal Island off Los Angeles, where Scott O'Dell was born. "Los Angeles was a frontier town when I was born there around the turn of the century," he wrote. "It had more horses than automobiles, more jackrabbits than people. The very first sound I remember was a wildcat scratching on the roof as I lay in bed."

I think you'll be surprised by the ending. Karana did some real tough things to survive. She sure is one brave woman. The last couple of lines were the most shocking to me, but I don't want to spoil it for you. As they say, never read the last page first.

Seth Anderson, Grade 5
Port Jefferson, New York

Streams to the River, River to the Sea

by Scott O'Dell

176 pages

This exciting story is about Sacagawea (sa-ka-ja-WAY-ah), an Indian princess. She is to join the famous Lewis and Clark expedition by canoe from St. Louis, Missouri, to the Pacific Ocean.

I learned many things about the expedition and Native Americans. I don't think I could have survived very long in that world, nor could many people of today because we don't know how to hunt for food or make our clothes. All we know how to do is go to the grocery store!

This book is historical fiction. The characters seem real because none of them is perfect. I think ten-year-olds to adults will enjoy this book.

Rebecca Bryant, Grade 5
Goshen, Kentucky

Oceanarium

by Joanne Oppenheim

40 pages

ANIMAL

ENVIRONMENT

Want to see the whales from the ocean floor? *Oceanarium,* illustrated by Alan Gutierrez, is filled with pictures just like that. The author takes you on an elevator ride to the underwater world of adventure, through schools of fish and even a shark tank.

The shark tank is the most interesting, with some scary facts about sharks' razor-sharp teeth, and a drawing of their insides! Did you know that the color of a shark helps you to know where it lives?

If you enjoy all the creatures of the sea and want to learn more about the way they live, and to help save them, you'll want to be sure and "catch" this book!

**Nicole Hughes, Grade 3
Lynnwood, Washington**

Idea Factory

Q. Where do writers get their ideas?
A. Everywhere!
Serious writers keep idea files or notebooks. You can, too. Get a pack of 3-by-5 notecards or a notebook small enough to carry with you everywhere. Whenever you come across something interesting—that you've read, thought, overheard, seen—write it down. Immediately!

The Island on Bird Street

by Uri Orlev

176 pages

CHALLENGE/
COURAGE

HISTORY

A good book to read is *The Island on Bird Street*. It is about a brave eleven-year-old boy named Alex and what he must do to survive during World War II. Alex's father is taken by the German army. Alex and his pet mouse, Snow, are left alone and forced to live in an empty building with little food or water, all the time hiding from the Germans. This book is sad because so many people were mistreated and killed. I recommend it highly if you enjoy reading about courage and bravery.

**Ryan Somers, Grade 4
Milltown, New Jersey**

Check It Out!

If you're moved by the plight of Alex in *The Island on Bird Street,* read *Anne Frank, The Diary of a Young Girl,* the true story of a child told in her own words. She and her family hid from the Germans during World War II for more than two years, but were sent to a concentration camp. See the review on page 79.

The Mystery of Chimney Rock
(Choose Your Own Adventure #5)

by Edward Packard

118 pages

ADVENTURE

MYSTERY

If you are the type that likes to choose your own destiny, then try a *Choose Your Own Adventure* book. *The Mystery of Chimney Rock* takes you on several adventures through an old deserted stone house in Connecticut.

In my favorite adventure you find an iron ring connected to a wooden floor. You pull the ring and POP!! A trapdoor opens, leading down circular steps to an unknown place. You start walking down the steps and Bang!! The trapdoor closes. Now you can choose your own destiny. #1—you can continue down the steps or #2—you can go back up the stairs to make sure that you can still open the trapdoor.

I liked the author's writing because I am adventurous, and this book has a lot of excitement. Edward Packard is probably very adventurous himself.

The book made me feel I was in charge. It made me feel that way because at some points you can choose your own path. A fun thing I learned from this book is that you never know where you might end up.

··········**Adam Mihalik, Grade 3**
Wantagh, New York

Merry Christmas, Amelia Bedelia

by Peggy Parish

64 pages

HUMOR

I like this book because it is very funny. In part of it Amelia Bedilia had to make a date cake, and she put dates in it from a calendar. In another part she had to put balls on the Christmas tree and she put sports balls on it. When she had to put the star on the tree, she put a mirror on the tree and a sign that said, "See the star." Amelia Bedelia is a real character! I think you will like this book.

Julia Schwartz, Grade 2
Port Jefferson, New York

Operation Dump the Chump

by Barbara Park

128 pages

ADVENTURE

HUMOR

I recently finished reading *Operation Dump the Chump*. It was very good! The main character is a twelve-year-old boy named Oscar Winkle. I liked Oscar because he thinks up a plan called "Operation Dump the Chump" to get rid of his pesky brother, Robert Winkle, for the summer. Robert is very bad and does awful things to Oscar. The characters reminded me of my brother and me. Lots of times we have trouble getting along together, but he's never pulled any tricks as bad as Robert's.

The book did leave me with something to think about. It gave me an idea of how to get rid of my brother for the summer! I think you should read this book because it is very funny!

Tara Mabry, Grade 3
La Mesa, California

Top Five Ways to Find a Good Book

5. Read book review.
4. Read over someone's shoulder. (But don't let him or her catch you!)
3. Check out the award winners at the library or bookstore.
2. Ask a friend, parent, librarian, or teacher.
1. Read this book!

Inside Dinosaurs and Other Prehistoric Creatures

by Stephen Parker

48 pages

ANIMAL

ENVIRONMENT

This book is about the insides of dinosaurs. It has interesting pictures of bones and muscles. It even shows how a dinosaur lays eggs. One funny picture shows a baby growing in the egg and sleeping on a bed. On the last page, there is a graph that shows dinosaurs on the slide to extinction. I liked this book because it has many neat facts.

Christopher J. Scott, Grade 3
Winnipeg, Manitoba, Canada

Big for Christmas
(Sweet Valley Twins & Friends #3)

by Francine Pascal

`256 pages`

ADVENTURE

FRIENDSHIP & FAMILY

When You Wish Upon a Star

Aesop said it 2,500 years ago—
"We would often be sorry if our wishes were gratified." It's been a theme in literature ever since. How do you think you would handle it if your wildest dreams came true? Do you imagine everything would be perfect? Might there be a down side?

Big for Christmas is about identical twins named Elizabeth and Jessica Wakefield and their extraordinary adventure. Elizabeth is the sensible and honest twin, but Jessica is the opposite; she is outgoing and wild.

Their parents refuse to let them go to a high school party because they're only in sixth grade. At the Christmas wishing well, they both wish to be bigger. The next day, they wake up to find themselves adults! Will anyone recognize them? Will they survive as adults? Find out by reading this excellent book.

I loved *Big for Christmas* because it was interesting and exciting. I liked certain parts, such as how they did their jobs and drove a car. When I read the book I felt as if I was watching, and I experienced how they felt. I recommend it to girls everywhere because it shows you what life is like when you are a grown-up. In the book you learn it through Elizabeth and Jessica's eyes. Boy, is it amazing!

**Christine Fahey, Grade 5
Bronx, New York**

The Haunted House
(Sweet Valley Twins #3)

by Francine Pascal

`112 pages`

ADVENTURE

FRIENDSHIP & FAMILY

Nora Mercandy lives in a mansion. People think it's haunted because every day Nora wears only black; plus her hair is also black. People play tricks on her and make fun of her. Then Nora dares the Sweet Valley Unicorn Club to come prove that her house isn't haunted.

This book made me feel a little sad, especially when everybody was being mean to Nora and never believed the things she said. I liked the part when the people found out that her mansion wasn't haunted.

I recommend this book because it teaches you a very good lesson; Don't judge people by what they look like. I think this is a great book, and I recommend you read it sometime.

**Alyson Holland, Grade 5
Hubert, North Carolina**

Where the Bald Eagles Gather

by Dorothy H. Patent

ANIMAL

ENVIRONMENT

This excellent nonfiction book is about the bald eagle's life. It tells about where the bald eagles live and what kinds of food they eat. It explains how scientists use bald eagles in their experiments. I liked this book because I found out interesting information about bald eagles. They sure are cool creatures!

Christan Henderson, Grade 4 Arlington, Virginia

Fine Feathered Facts

▼ Ben Franklin didn't think the bald eagle should be our national symbol. He wanted that honor for the turkey!

▼ Bald eagles are skilled fishers, but they'd rather steal another bird's catch than find their own. (This was one of Ben's objections to the choice!)

▼ Bald eagles build a new nest every year, often right on top of last year's. Sometimes they do this over and over—until the tree collapses

Which would you vote for: a bald eagle, a turkey, or another bird?

Bridge to Terabithia

by Katherine Paterson

CHALLENGE/ COURAGE

DRAMA

FRIENDSHIP & FAMILY

Author: Katherine Paterson

Katherine Paterson has written many exciting novels. One of my favorites is *Bridge to Terabithia*. It tells about how a boy, Jesse Oliver Aarons, Jr., and a girl, Leslie Burke's friendship begins, develops, and changes. They build a secret land called Terabithia. There they share their secrets and feelings. Then one day, something tragic happens. Will it have any effect on Terabithia?

This book made me feel I was right there with the characters; feeling their sadness, laughing with them, and feeling each other's joys. This proves that the writer is really good.

This book reminds me of my friends, always looking for adventure, wanting to create this and that. A book that reminds you of you and your friends is like having a book about yourself on the shelf.

I recommend this book to many young readers who like adventure, sadness, and just plain old fun. *Bridge to Terabithia* is exciting. I'm sure you'll love it.

Stephanie Carter, Grade 5 Berea, Kentucky

The Great Gilly Hopkins

by Katherine Paterson

192 pages

CHALLENGE/ COURAGE

DRAMA

FRIENDSHIP & FAMILY

The Great Gilly Hopkins is by Katherine Paterson. I liked and disliked Gilly, the main character. I liked her because she was smart and independent. I disliked her because she stole money and was ugly to people. Gilly also did not like anyone and she did not want anyone to like her.

This book made me think about how important families are. Gilly is a foster child and did not have a family. Not having a family made Gilly have some bad qualities.

In the beginning of the book, Gilly is being sent to a new foster home. Later in the book, Gilly tries to find her mother but does not succeed. At the end of the book, Gilly meets her mother, but the meeting is a disappointment.

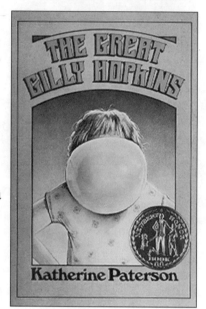

The Great Gilly Hopkins is a great book for all ages.

**Douglas Swords, Grade 5
Waxhaw, North Carolina**

The River Dragon

by Darcy Pattison

32 pages

ADVENTURE

FANTASY & FOLKLORE

MULTICULTURAL

The book, *The River Dragon*, by Darcy Pattison, made me feel curious because I wondered what would happen next. I like the main character, Ying Shao, because he is brave and confident. The artwork is very good—even the dragon looks real! I would not change this book one bit because it is so suspenseful and well written. This book also tells what the Chinese believe in. It taught me about the Chinese culture. I highly recommend the book to any Chinese fans or any people who want to learn about the Chinese culture.

**Linsay Read, Grade 4
Everton, Arkansas**

Hatchet

by Gary Paulsen   208 pages

Do you like exciting adventure stories? If you do, you should read *Hatchet*. It's about a boy named Brian Robinson who lives through a plane crash and learns how to survive in the wilderness. Brian is tremendously resourceful. He learns to start a fire and keep it going for months! He makes a bow and arrow to help him hunt and fish. He learns how to cook the birds, fish, and rabbits he catches.

I was interested in learning about survival. This book taught me that I can do anything if I try hard enough and use my head. I learned that I could survive in the wilderness for a long time if I had food, shelter, and a hatchet to use. I really enjoyed reading *Hatchet*. It is the best book I have ever read...unless the sequel, *The River,* is even better!

Ben Smith, Grade 5
Land O'Lakes, Florida

Hatchet

by Gary Paulsen   208 pages

Have you ever thought about being stranded alone in the middle of nowhere? Well, neither did Brian Robinson, the thirteen-year-old character in *Hatchet*.

That's exactly what happens to Brian when the private plane he's flying in crashes in the Canadian forest in the middle of a lake. Brian, the only survivor, is on his own without food or shelter. He must learn to survive in the wilderness with only the hatchet strapped to his belt.

I think this book is so great because Brian had the courage to try to survive. If you like adventure and suspense, this book's for you.

I discovered this book after seeing the movie, *A Cry in the Wild*. It was based on the book, *Hatchet*. The book is much better because it tells so much. There's a sequel to this book called *The River*. It's full of the same kind of excitement and suspense I found in *Hatchet*. If you read *Hatchet*, you have to read the sequel.

Jeff Pedersen, Grade 4
Littleton, Colorado

Check It Out!

Gary Paulsen's many novels have a common theme—people finding strength and confidence from the outdoors. If you liked *Hatchet,* you might try *Dogsong, Tracker,* and *The Voyage of the Frog.* In each of these novels, teenagers rise to meet challenges presented by nature. The author spent his own teens hunting, trapping, and camping in the Minnesota woods.

The Monument

by Gary Paulsen

160 pages

CHALLENGE/ COURAGE

ENVIRONMENT

FRIENDSHIP & FAMILY

This book is about a town in Ohio that wants a monument like the one in Washington to honor all the young men who served and died in Vietnam. The town needs someone to develop and pursue this idea, and they hire a young man named Nick. Nick's notion of art is different from the average person's. Art, he feels, is all about the past, present, and future. Nick figures the town needs something simple but unique. With pen in hand, Nick begins sketching the town. He decides that the beauty of nature—trees, flowers, etc.—will make a gorgeous monument, because it will be around forever as the city to grows and prospers.

This book is interesting because it is descriptive and it showed me art in a whole different way. Art is in everything, you just have to look hard enough. Many people think that art is just a picture or painting, but even we ourselves are art.

David Schor, Grade 5
Trumbull, Connecticut

The River

by Gary Paulsen

144 pages

ADVENTURE

CHALLENGE/ COURAGE

DRAMA

ENVIRONMENT

In *The River* by Gary Paulsen, Brian Robeson and Derek Holtzer go into the wilderness to try to survive. In the first book, *Hatchet,* Brian crashes in a plane and survives in the wilderness for 54 days. Now, Derek Holtzer, a government psychologist, wants him to do it again. Every move, action, and word Brian says, Derek writes down. That is, until Derek gets hit by lightning. If he hadn't reached up for the radio, the accident would never have happened. To make matters worse, now the radio is dead. The only solution is for Brian to build a raft and go 100 miles down a river. Is the map is accurate? Will he make it? Read this gripping book to find out.

Sam Tremble, Grade 5
Cherry Hill, New Jersey

The Wild Culpepper Cruise

by Gary Paulsen

80 pages

ADVENTURE

FRIENDSHIP & FAMILY

HUMOR

Amos wins a "Why I Love My Dog" contest and he and his best friend for life, Dunc, go on a cruise ship through the Caribbean Sea. They get their bags mixed up with jewel thieves and find stolen jewels. Lots of other funny things happen on the ship, too. An older lady grabs Amos's hand and started dancing with him. During dance class he gets seasick, a wire tears his pants, and he ends up in a cake.

I liked the book because of what happens to Amos. Also, Amos is always getting in trouble. Amos never likes it when Dunc takes everything seriously. *The Wild Culpepper Cruise* is one hilarious book. Now read it yourself!

Nathaniel Cross, Grade 5
Ft. Madison, Iowa

**Author:
Gary Paulsen**

Unfinished Portrait of Jessica

by Richard Peck

176 pages

ADVENTURE

CHALLENGE/
COURAGE

Jessica goes to visit her father at her great-uncle's house in Mexico after her parents divorce. Jessica has imagined a perfect vacation. And her trip *does* turn out to be paradise, with Brooke, Tony, and the other Christmas guests. They all enjoy seeing the sights in Acapulco. Everything is wonderful, except Jessica has trouble getting along with her father, who is not the perfect parent she had imagined.

After her trip to Mexico, Jessica grows up and goes to college. She learns to accept her father not being with her and her mother as a person she loves and not her enemy. Then Jessica gets some bad news.

The author describes what happened to the characters after the main story is over. It is like a real person's life, and you can imagine everything about Jessica's story because the book is so realistic. The book is divided into two parts: Amor and Muerte, which mean love and death.

I would definitely recommend this book to others to read. It made me feel happy, sad, mad, anxious, and worried! *Unfinished Portrait of Jessica* is a very good book.

Rachel Ashton, Grade 6
Swansboro, North Carolina

Hangman

by John Peel

128 pages

FRIENDSHIP & FAMILY

THRILLS & CHILLS

Hangman by John Peel is a very scary book. It's about three girls who have a sleepover. They begin telling stories about a man who got hanged for killing his family. But he didn't really do it. Then spookey things start happening. A dog from next door dies, and frightening hangman games start to appear in strange places. I really like this book because it's scary and I like scary stuff! When I was reading it, I felt really frightened. I think anybody who likes scary movies should read this book. Just one tip: Don't read it alone at night!

John McCaig, Grade 4
East Brunswick, New Jersey

Tituba of Salem Village

by Ann Petry

254 pages

DRAMA

HISTORY

If you want to read a great book, *Tituba of Salem Village* by Ann Petry is for you. In 1692, in Salem Village, Massachusetts, many people are talking about witches and magic. Someone in the village has been doing very bad things. Everyone thinks it is Tituba, the minister's slave, because she can tell fortunes and do many other magical things. A witch-hunt begins in Salem! I like this book because it is based on a true story.

Bridget McKeon, Grade 5
Hamden, Connecticut

When Fiction Becomes Fact

Readers enjoy being spooked by scary stories, such as *Hangman*. Sometimes people in real life allow themselves to be overcome by a groundless fear. In *Tituba of Salem Village*, a community lets their imagination take control of their senses, with horrible consequences.

Sister of the Quints

by Stella Pevsner

192 pages

CHALLENGE/
COURAGE

FRIENDSHIP
& FAMILY

I think that *Sister of the Quints* is a wonderful book. It is about a girl named Natalie who cannot escape from her five identical baby brothers and sisters. They not only tear up the entire house, but they are keeping their family apart as well. Natalie's mother and father are making her stay home and baby-sit instead of going to soccer practice. Natalie thinks that she has her own life to live, until one of her sisters is missing and Natalie becomes aware of her true feelings about "the quints." I really enjoyed this book because it tells what being a family is all about.

**Olga Kegnian, Grade 6
Bronx, New York**

The Rainbow Fish

by Marcus Pfister

32 pages

ANIMAL

FRIENDSHIP
& FAMILY

The Rainbow Fish is a wonderful book that teaches you not to think about yourself all the time, but to think about other people, too. It also teaches that you should share your most prized possessions, like the rainbow fish, with others. Don't be greedy! This book has outstanding pictures. The rainbow colors and the silver touch really add to the book. This book made me feel great when I read it. I would definitely, with a capital *D*, recommend this book to everybody, even adults. This is one of the BEST books I've ever read.

**Lauren Wilson, Grade 3
Summerville, South Carolina**

Author! Illustrator!

Marcus Pfister, a Swiss writer-illustrator, is known for his books that feature holographic foil, like *The Rainbow Fish*. First, Pfister perfects his story. Then, he paints with wet watercolor on wet paper for a soft effect. He adds details after the paintings dry. Finally, he shows on an overlay where the foil should go. A machine applies the special foil to the printed illustrations.

The Midnight Club

by Christopher Pike

256 pages

FRIENDSHIP & FAMILY

THRILLS & CHILLS

The Midnight Club is their name, and telling stories is their game.

The Midnight Club is about five teenagers who all have an incurable disease. They all live in the Rotterham Home hospice, where those who check in don't check out! To make the best out of the situation, they meet every night and tell stories: violent stories, romance stories, true stories, false stories, stories of many different kinds.

I really liked the book because of the way the author tells the story; it is very captivating and some parts are touching. The book makes me feel so lucky to have all that I have now, for the characters in the story barely have their lives to live. It also makes me think what will happen when we die. Do we have another life after this?

I would recommend this moving book to people who are interested in life after death. You just might learn something from it. To know more about the stories, read *The Midnight Club*.

> **Patty Wu, Grade 7**
> **Hsinchu, Taiwan**

Thirteen

edited by Tonya Pines

304 pages

THRILLS & CHILLS

MYSTERY

This is a book with thirteen short stories by thirteen awesome horror story writers like R. L. Stine, Christopher Pike, Diane Hoh, and Carol Ellis. Christopher Pike has a two-part story titled "Collect Call." It is the first and the last story in the book, so it leaves you hanging until the end. R. L. Stine's story "The Spell" is about a kid who hypnotizes another kid. The results are deadly. A story by Carol Ellis is called "The Doll." It is about a girl who finds a doll in the attic and dreams about it. Then terrible things start happening to her friends. "House of Horrors" by J. B. Stamper is about some kids who work in a wax museum. They trick a boy by planning a party in the museum after it closes. No one shows up but him. He is left alone in the museum. Can you imagine what happened to him that night?

These stories will keep you up for the next year. So, if you would like a good scare, read this book . . . and show 'em you're not afraid!

> **John Wozniak, Grade 5**
> **Andover, New Jersey**

Lizard Music

by D. Manus Pinkwater

160 pages

Lizard Music by D. Manus Pinkwater is a wonderful adventure. It's about a ten-year-old boy named Victor who is left alone by his older sister when their parents go on vacation. She was supposed to watch him. When everyone is gone, Victor goes on many adventures and meets many people, like The Chicken Man. The Chicken Man takes Victor to a wonderful island where lizards are living. Read this book to find out how this changes Victor's life forever. I really liked this book because it is so funny. I very much recommend it to everyone who loves to laugh.

Author: D. Manus Pinkwater

**Krissy Neumann, Grade 4
Darien, Illinois**

The Shadowman's Way

by Paul Pitts

128 pages

The Shadowman's Way is about a Biligaana (white man) named Spencer West and a Navajo boy named Nelson Sam. When Spencer comes to his first day of school, he gets humiliated by something he said. Another Navajo boy named Benjamin Nez teases Nelson because he likes the white man. I won't tell you any more. If you want to find out what happened, read *The Shadowman's Way*. I liked this book because it was exciting. It taught me not to tease people because they are different.

**James Baldesweiler, Grade 4
East Brunswick, New Jersey**

A Writer's Corner

Inspired to write? Make yourself a studio. Include:

1. **Desk and chair.** A clipboard and cushion will do.
2. **Paper.** All sorts, lined and unlined.
3. **Writing instruments.** Pens, pencils, a computer or word processor, if possible.
4. **Office supplies.** Paper clips, stapler, tape, glue stick, stamps, envelopes.
5. **Bulletin board.** Tack up ideas, quotes, pictures, anything to jump-start your creativity!

147

Ten Great Mysteries

by Edgar Allan Poe

236 pages

THRILLS & CHILLS

MYSTERY

This book is a collection of stories by the famous writer, Edgar Allan Poe. His stories are horror tales, mostly having to do with death.

"The Descent Into the Maelstrom" is a story about a man and his family going down a whirlpool. The man notices that cylinders go down the whirlpool much slower. With this knowledge, he gets a barrel and escapes the whirlpool, while his family, refusing to go with him, drowns.

I liked all the stories, but my favorite was "The Pit and the Pendulum." This story is about a man who was sentenced to death and put in a square prison. In the middle there was a pit filled with water. When he escaped the pit, he got tied to a bench with a pendulum swinging over him, each time getting a little lower. When he escaped the pendulum, the walls moved together and squished into the shape of a lozenge, encouraging him to jump into the pit. Just as he jumped into the pit, a hand reached down and grabbed him out of the prison.

I recommend this book for ages ten and up because the words Poe uses might be a little hard for people under ten.

Christopher Tibbs, Grade 4
Millville, New Jersey

Babushka's Doll

by Patricia Polacco

40 pages

FANTASY & FOLKLORE

FRIENDSHIP & FAMILY

This story takes you on a wild adventure. *Babushka's Doll* is about a selfish little girl named Natasha who asks her grandmother to do hard work, like giving her a ride in the goat cart.

When Natasha sees a pretty doll on a shelf, she asked if she may play with it. Grandma says, "Yes, but I only played with her once." While grandma is at the store, the little doll pops up and makes Natasha work for her, like pushing her in the goat cart! The little doll gives Natasha a big lesson, and in the end she turns out to be a pretty good girl! This book sort of gave me the spooks, but it's a good lesson!

Tara Lundie, Grade 3
Port Jefferson, New York

Chicken Sunday

by Patricia Polacco

Do you like chicken? Well if you do, *Chicken Sunday* by Patricia Polacco is the right book for you. It's about three kids: Stewart, Winston, and the little girl. They worked to buy the glorious hat in the hat shop, which their grandmother admired. I liked this book and recommend it for everybody because it warmed my heart and was so exciting I could die.

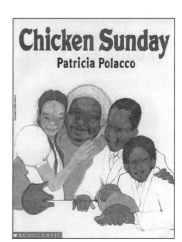

Anne Zeumer, Grade 2
Port Jefferson, New York

Picnic at Mudsock Meadow

by Patricia Polacco

This story takes place in the country and in two tepees. It reminded me of last Halloween when I got scared. The lesson it taught me is: We shouldn't be afraid of scary shadows. Here's what happens in the book: At the end of the picnic William saw a light and everybody went outside. Then everybody saw a very scary thing heading toward them, but then it stopped. Before it stopped they all ran inside. William was the only one outside. He was afraid, but he went to the swamp to see what it was. It was a mouse, but William didn't know. So he jumped in the

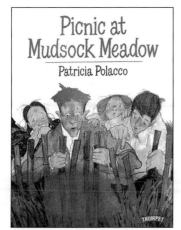

water to see what it was. When William came out of the swamp, he was muddy. Then he won first place because he had the scariest Halloween costume. The end.

What I noticed about Patricia Polacco's writing is it is very interesting. I loved the book and I recommend it to other kids.

Samantha Koutrakos, Grade 3
Port Jefferson, New York

Thunder Cake

by Patricia Polacco

32 pages

CHALLENGE/ COURAGE

FRIENDSHIP & FAMILY

Thunder Cake is very interesting. It's about a little girl who was frightened of storms, especially thunderstorms. But her babushka (that means "grandma") said, "don't be afraid." So they made a very special cake called thunder cake. It is a very difficult cake to make. The girl went through many obstacles. When they made the cake the girl was not afraid. The lesson is: Don't be afraid of a storm. I recommend this book to other kids because you will never know what happens next!

**Gary Vegliante, Grade 2
Port Jefferson, New York**

Author: Patricia Polacco

Keep on Rockin'

Patricia Polacco has a dozen rocking chairs in her home. She rocks to gather her thoughts, recall stories told her by "the old folks"—her grandparents from Russia—and to come up with stories on her own. In fact, psychologists have found that the motion of rocking helps stimulate the parts of the brain related to memory.

Meet Addy

by Connie Porter

69 pages

CHALLENGE/ COURAGE

DRAMA

HISTORY

This book is about slavery and freedom. It is about a nine-year-old girl named Addy who lives on a plantation in the midst of the Civil War. I really recommend this book to everyone, boys or girls, because it tells you about history and it's very interesting. The illustrations are great! They show certain scenes from the book, and they are clear and colorful. I learned a lot of facts in a section at the back of the book called "Looking Back 1864: A peek into the past." This book made me feel sad and ashamed of the U.S.A., because the white people treated black people like "things." I'm glad slavery has ended, but things are still not perfect.

Angeline Grace Gragasin, Grade 4
Racine, Wisconsin

Something BIG Has Been Here

by Jack Prelutsky

HUMOR

POETRY

Author:
Jack Prelutsky

I think this book should be for ages seven to any adult. I think the author and illustrator worked very hard to create these poems for kids. And I would like to see more of Jack Prelutsky's great funny poems. He writes about a lot of things. His poems seem like fiction. There are two poems I like the best. They are called "The Turkey Shot Out of the Oven" and "I am Growing a Glorious Garden." These two poems are the best in the whole book because they made me laugh and laugh.

**Spenser Williams, Grade 2
Port Jefferson, New York**

The Golden Days

by Gail Radley

ADVENTURE

**CHALLENGE/
COURAGE**

**FRIENDSHIP
& FAMILY**

This story is about a friendship between a seventy-five-year-old lady named Carlotta and an eleven-year-old boy named Cory. Carlotta used to work in the circus as a fortune teller and is now in a nursing home. Cory is in fourth grade and has been moved from foster home to foster home. Cory and Carlotta seem like total opposites. But when they get to know each other, they find out that they are a lot alike. They both want to move. They want to live together, but can they survive on their own? You should read this book if you want to find out what happens. I liked this book because it is really exciting. There is only one thing wrong with it: The beginning is boring.

Cody Agans, Grade 4
Decatur, Illinois

Between Two Worlds

by Candice Ransom

160 pages

CHALLENGE/
COURAGE

DRAMA

FRIENDSHIP
& FAMILY

MULTICULTURAL

Between Two Worlds is a true story about Sarah, a Paiute girl, when American soldiers were against Indians. I like it because it has happy, sad, adventurous, and scary parts. A sad and scary part is when Sarah's baby brother got thrown into a fire by soldiers. If that happened to me, I would have an icy spot in my heart and nothing could melt the ice. An adventurous part is when Sarah and her tribe walk all the way from Nevada to California to meet their white brothers. Sarah was shy because she had never met a white person. A happy part is when Sarah goes to go to school and learns to read and write.

Sarah was caught between two worlds because she wanted to visit many whites and help them learn about Indians. But half of her family wanted nothing to do with them.

The book only has one black-and-white picture—a photo of Sarah—near the front. It is a chapter book. I really recommend this book because it taught me about how Indians felt and thought, and what some white people thought about and did to Indians.

**Amber Egbert, Grade 3
Anderson, Indiana**

The Westing Game

by Ellen Raskin

192 pages

MYSTERY

The Westing Game takes place in Wisconsin off the Lake Michigan coast. The characters are 16 heirs who live in a new apartment complex across the street from the estate of the late Samuel W. Westing.

The heirs gather at the estate for the reading of the will. They are surprised to find the will to be a game challenging the heirs to find Westing's murderer. The heirs track down clue after clue, not realizing the murderer could be one of them. Will they catch the murderer before he or she strikes again? Or will evil triumph? To find out, read!

I liked *The Westing Game,* especially because it makes you one of the heirs and gives you a chance to solve the mind-boggling puzzle before the end of the book. I love mysteries, and I have found none better than *The Westing Game.*

**Josh Patashnik, Grade 4
San Diego, California**

Where the Red Fern Grows

by Wilson Rawls

208 pages

ADVENTURE

ANIMAL

FRIENDSHIP & FAMILY

This story is about a young boy, Billy, who wants a pair of hound puppies so much that he works two years to get them. Billy is one of the most determined people I have ever read about. When he puts his heart into getting those dogs, his heart does not wander.

I learned that loyalty, trust, and love are not only human traits. Billy's dogs love each other and they love Billy as well. This book also helped me understand how hard it was for some people to live in the hills of the Ozark Mountains. They did not have many of the things I take for granted.

My mother also loved this book, so there is no age limit for enjoying *Where the Red Fern Grows*.

Alexandra Dean Barnes, Grade 5
Sylva, North Carolina

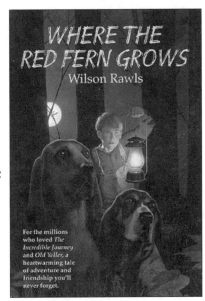

Sharks: Silent Hunters of the Deep

by Reader's Digest

208 pages

ANIMAL

ENVIRONMENT

Did you know, if you rub a shark with your bare hand you would get cut badly; the smallest shark can fit in the palm of your hand, and the leopard shark really has spots? I found all of this out by reading *Sharks: Silent Hunters of the Deep*. This book tells you tales, facts, and true stories about sharks. I found this a very interesting book to read because I love sharks and I have been studying them for six years. This book helped me, and it might help you too.

Luke Fraley, Grade 4
Washington Depot,
Connecticut

Shared Reading

There's nothing like a great book—except sharing it! Here's how:

1. **Read aloud.** Make it part of your family's daily routine.
2. **Start a book discussion group.** Ask a librarian or teacher to help.
3. **Read to someone who can't.** Check out *The Kid's Guide to Service Projects* by Barbara Lewis to find an audience who will appreciate a reader.

The Magic Amber

retold by Charles Reasoner

`32 pages`

ADVENTURE

FANTASY & FOLKLORE

MULTICULTURAL

The Magic Amber is a neatly told legend about an old, poor couple who are kind to a stranger. In return, the stranger gives the couple a magic amber stone that gives them tons of rice. However, the stone gets stolen! You'll want to see what happens next to the kind old couple and the thief.

I love this story because it is from Korea, the place where I was born. The old couple reminds me of my parents, who are so kind to me and I am kind to them. The artwork in the book is beautiful. I learned from this book that you will get back the kindness you give.

If you like legends from around the world, you will like this book.

Hunter Clark, Grade 5
Anderson, South Carolina

A Little Bit Dead

by Chap Reaver

`192 pages`

DRAMA

FRIENDSHIP & FAMILY

MULTICULTURAL

This story is about an eighteen-year-old boy named Reece who stopped three men who were whipping an Indian. Then two of the men murdered the other one and said that Reece had shot him. The Indian Reece had met pays a price to save Reece's life. The rest of the story is about what happens to Reece and the Indian.

What I liked about the story was that the author wrote the dialogue so that it sounded like a real person. This was not correct English; it was how someone would normally talk. For example, they would always say 'cause, and they all had an accent.

In the story, the white men had more fights than the Indians. It reminded me of equal rights for all races. I especially thought it was stupid because white men could own land and Indians could not.

I recommend this book to others because it is well written and exciting. I really enjoyed the part about the friendship between Reece and the Indian, Shanti.

Jeremy H. Curtiss, Grade 4
Erdenheim, Pennsylvania

Check It Out!

It's not always easy to do the right thing, especially when others don't. If you liked this book, you may also enjoy *The Light in the Forest* by Conrad Richter. A frontier boy struggles with the hatred on both sides as he lives first with his family and later with the Indians who capture him. Find out if he does the right thing, too.

Shades of Gray

by Carolyn Reeder

After the Civil War, a boy named Will travels to the Virginia Piedmont to live with his aunt and uncle following the death of his family. Adjusting to his new life on the farm, Will must face many hard challenges. Will is bullied, poor, and misses his old city life. Most of all, Will must learn to hunt and farm from his uncle, who refuses to fight, even in the Civil War.

I enjoyed this book for the choices that the characters had to make: Uncle Jed's choice, to fight or not to fight, and Will's choice, to return to an easy life in the city or to stay with his new family. Read this book and find out what choices they made and how they decided.

Andrew Ryley, Grade 5
Waterville, Ohio

Home for the Howl-idays

by Dian Curtis Regan

Do you like monsters? Well, if you do, you will like *Home for the Howl-idays.* Aleesa and her brother, Sam, come home for the holidays, but when they get there, they realize that their family has turned into monsters! Their mother is a mummy; their father is a vampire; their brother a werewolf; their butler is Frankenstein; and their grandmother is a ghost!

Not only was their family transformed into monsters, but when they sit down to eat dinner, most of the time their food slithers away!

I liked the ending, but I don't want to spoil it for you. I definitely recommend this book to anyone who likes monsters and the Christmas Howl-idays!

Jenna Gwaltney, Grade 3
Raleigh, North Carolina

Three of a Kind

by Louise Rich

164 pages

CHALLENGE/ COURAGE

FRIENDSHIP & FAMILY

Cat, Becka, and Josie are the oldest girls at Willoughby Hall Home for Children. They have been together for years. Each of them has a desperate wish: to have a real family and real parents. Then a couple named Annie and Ben Morgan appear, looking for a daughter. Will the girls be separated? Will the Morgans want a different girl? Well, to find out, read *Three of a Kind*.

This book made me feel very glad to have a family. I recommend it to others because I thiink it is a great book and I want everyone else to feel this greatness.

**Mary Weihe, Grade 5
Bronx, New York**

Friedrich

by Hans Peter Richter

128 pages

CHALLENGE/ COURAGE

DRAMA

FRIENDSHIP & FAMILY

HISTORY

Friedrich is a great book about a Jewish boy living while Hitler was in power. Hitler was the Nazi leader in Germany. Hitler deprived Jews of their rights and made many people think the Jews were the cause of their problems. When Friedrich's mother dies and his father is sent to a concentration camp, Friedrich is left an orphan.

The author, Hans Peter Richter, lived in Germany during the Third Reich. The Third Reich was Hitler's government. What made this book really good was that it was told from a kid's point of view.

I recommend this book to people who would like to learn how it was to be a Jew in World War II. I not only recommend this book to kids, I would recommend it to people of all ages. This book makes you realize that something like that could happen today.

If I had to rate this book on a scale of one to ten, I would easily give it a ten.

**Jacob Colombo, Grade 5
Weare, New Hampshire**

To Space and Back

by Sally Ride with Susan Okie

ADVENTURE

ENVIRONMENT

You think this book is about something on Earth? No!! It's about what it is like to be inside a space shuttle in space. *To Space and Back* has photographs that will make you want to go into space too. They show what it is like to work inside a shuttle. If you like space, this book is for you.

**Christopher Scotton, Grade 2
Lynnwood, Washington**

Author:
Sally Ride

Don't Hurt Laurie!

by Willo Davis Roberts

CHALLENGE/
COURAGE

DRAMA

FRIENDSHIP
& FAMILY

Don't Hurt Laurie! by Willo Davis Roberts is a really emotional book. It is about an eleven-year-old girl who has been keeping a secret for as long as she can remember—a secret that she is afraid to tell anyone.

The only other person who knows Laurie's secret is Anabelle, Laurie's mom, because she is the one who is beating Laurie. Anabelle always tries to find a way to hurt Laurie, and one day Laurie finally is desperate to get away from her mother, but she has one problem: how? This is a really heartwarming book that I would be eager to read again.

**Vaishaly Shah, Grade 5
Houston, Texas**

Storytelling

Want to make a story you love come alive? Try telling it! To get started:

1. **Choose the right story.** Fairy tales, fables, and your own stories are good.
2. **Dramatize.** Use sound effects, "voices," gestures, props.
3. **Rehearse.** Use a mirror, tape recorder, and practice audiences.
4. **Start telling!** For more help, read *The Storyteller's Start-up Book* by Margaret Read MacDonald.

Sugar Isn't Everything

by Willo Davis Roberts

192 pages

CHALLENGE/COURAGE

DRAMA

In *Sugar Isn't Everything,* a ten-year-old named Amy starts feeling horrible all the time. She is always hungry and thirsty, no matter how much she eats or drinks. One day, she collapses and is rushed to the hospital. It turns out that she has diabetes. While Amy is in the hospital, she sees what happens if you don't follow the rules of being a diabetic. Later in the book, Amy helps save a friend who also has diabetes.

The author, Willo Davis Roberts, has diabetes herself and knows the struggle of diabetics, their families, and friends. If you are a diabetic, this will help you understand that you are not the only one. This will help everyone understand how a friendship can fade. I recommend this book to anyone who has a best friend.

**Sarah Loring, Grade 5
Columbia, Missouri**

Finding Support

In *Sugar Isn't Everything,* Amy finds that talking to other people with diabetes helps her understand and accept her illness. Today, it is possible to find a support group for almost any kind of problem. If you want more information about diabetes, you can call the Juvenile Diabetes Foundation's toll-free hot line (1-800-JDF-CURE). They can put you in touch with a support group in your area.

How to Eat Fried Worms

by Thomas Rockwell

128 pages

FRIENDSHIP & FAMILY

HUMOR

In this book Billy makes a bet that he can eat 15 worms in 15 days for $50. Then it's a battle between Billy and his friends, Alan and Joe, to see who will be the winner.

I'm glad I'm not Billy. I would never make a bet like that, because $50 is too much money to bet and eating worms is disgusting. I feel sick just thinking about it. I also see what happens when good friends bet money. Alan and Joe try every mean thing they can think of to win the $50.

I wouldn't want my friends to be so mean to me. I recommend this book to anyone with a strong stomach.

**Greg Diller, Grade 4
Mohegan Lake, New York**

Squishy Business

Did you know that some creatures have backbones and others don't? Cats, dogs, mice, people, deer, elephants, frogs, fish, snakes, and birds all have a backbone as well as other bones to protect and support their bodies. Worms, like grasshoppers, crayfish, starfish, and many others, do not.

Jim Abbott

by John Rolfe

144 pages

BIOGRAPHY

CHALLENGE/ COURAGE

SPORTS

If you like biographies and have a dream, *Jim Abbott* by John Rolfe is for you. It's my favorite! Jim Abbott was a determined young boy who played baseball with one normal arm and one arm that was deformed. I learned that just because someone is handicapped, it doesn't mean he cannot succeed in life. If you read this book, you will feel the challenges he came upon. I highly recommend this book to everyone!

**Aaron Feldman, Grade 5
Tampa, Florida**

When I Was Young in the Mountains

by Cynthia Rylant

32 pages

CHALLENGE/ COURAGE

ENVIRONMENT

FRIENDSHIP & FAMILY

When I Was Young in the Mountains is a book about a girl named Cynthia Rylant. She lived with her grandparents and other relatives in a four-room house in the mountains of Cool Ridge, West Virginia. They learned to make do with things they found in the mountains.

The closeness the people had for one another made me feel that growing up in the mountains was very special. This book has very happy paintings that show a family's love for one another. If you like to read books that make you feel good, I recommend this book to you.

**Lindsey LaPlant, Grade 5
Deerfield, Wisconsin**

Author: Cynthia Rylant

Amelia Earhart: Adventure in the Sky

by Francene Sabin

48 pages

BIOGRAPHY

CHALLENGE/ COURAGE

HISTORY

Do you like reading biographies? I do, and that's why I read *Amelia Earhart* by Francine Sabin. The book is about Amelia's life when she was young. Before she moved, Amelia got into trouble for playing with some friends. You should see the trouble she got in! The saddest part is when the plane Amelia was flying disappeared over the Pacific Ocean. *Amelia Earhart* is a great book to read, and I hope you enjoy it! It is fun to read biographies because you learn about famous people.

**Melissa Ciriello, Grade 4
East Brunswick,
New Jersey**

Practice Makes Perfect

Illustrators make practice books, called *dummies,* before doing final artwork. Here's how to make one:

1. Fold 8 pieces of paper in half. (This makes 32 pages, the length of most picture books.)
2. Staple or sew the pages together.
3. Divide your text among the pages. Remember "frontmatter" (title page, dedication).
4. Add illustrations. Make the pictures tell a story too!

Sideways Stories From Wayside School

by Louis Sachar

128 pages

HUMOR

Sideways Stories From Wayside School is totally hilarious! It was the book for me. I liked when the teacher, Ms. Gorf, wiggled her ears—first her right ear, then her left one—and then stuck out her tongue. She turned the kids into apples. But she's in for it when a mirror turns the magic back on her. The book made me remember when I tried doing magic. I didn't get the hang of it at all! This book is so fun to read. You'll never want to stop.

**Farrukh M. Hussain, Grade 4
Houston, Texas**

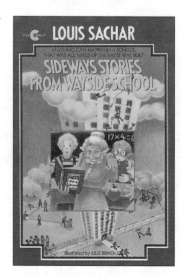

There's a Boy in the Girls' Bathroom

by Louis Sachar

208 pages

A kid named Bradley Chalkers is the tallest kid in fifth grade. He picks fights with everyone. He tells big lies. The only person who likes him is Carla. She's the new student counselor. She thinks he is sensitive and generous. She knows that Bradley can change. But Bradley isn't really sure. Sometimes the hardest thing to do is to believe in yourself.

I liked this book because it is about believing in yourself.

Naomi Daniels, Grade 5
Huntington, New York

Grandfather's Journey

by Allen Say

32 pages

Are you interested in your family's past? If you want to learn more about your ancestors, I would suggest you read *Grandfather's Journey*. This book tells about a man who sailed from Japan to California. Then he goes back to Japan, marries, and comes back to California, and has a daughter. When the daughter grows up, she goes to Japan with her family and marries. She then settles in a nearby city and has a boy. When the boy grows up, he comes to California, where he settles. But he visits Japan often and remembers his grandfather and the journey he took through his lifetime. This book helped me to inquire and learn about my family's heritage. I learned it really doesn't matter if people are white, black, Native American, or Asian. A family is a family no matter what culture you come from.

Heather Olson, Grade 4
Neenah, Wisconsin

Illustration Basics

Some tips for would-be illustrators:

1. **Learn to look.** Seeing how things really look is the heart of drawing well.
2. **Draw every day.** Most artists do.
3. **Experiment.** Try different ways of making lines, kinds of paint, collage, scratchboard, photography, print making.
4. **Examine books.** What do the illustrations add to the story? Try re-illustrating a book you love!

Knights of the Kitchen Table

by Jon Scieszka

64 pages

ADVENTURE

FANTASY & FOLKLORE

FRIENDSHIP & FAMILY

Had any good adventure with your friends lately? If you have (or if you haven't), read *Knights of the Kitchen Table*! It's about three good friends who go on many different, exciting adventures. This takes place at the kitchen table where the three boys are celebrating Joe's birthday. Joe got a magical gift from his uncle. When Joe opened his present, it took him and his two buddies on a journey back to the Knights of the Round Table. Anyone who ever loved magic and stories about dragons and giants would love this book.

**Albert Foley, Grade 4
Mahopac, New York**

Author! Author!
Although Jon Scieszka has always loved children, he originally wanted to write for adults. He changed his mind after becoming an elementary school teacher. He saw that kids loved to have well-known stories turned upside down. A favorite motto of his is, "Have fun and tell lots of bad jokes as often as possible."

The Stinky Cheese Man and Other Fairly Stupid Tales

by Jon Scieszka and Lane Smith

56 pages

FANTASY & FOLKLORE

HUMOR

This book is so funny you might fall off your chair reading it. The Stinky Cheese stunk so bad the cow that the man passed almost died because of the smell. The artwork is just grand, the expressions on the characters' faces are funny, and the drawings of the animals are great too. This book reminds me of Mother Goose stories like "The Princess and the Pea," but what makes it extra great is that the author mixed them up and changed them around to make them funny, like "The Princess and the Bowling Ball." So get *The Stinky Cheese Man* and read all his *Other Fairly Stupid Tales*.

**Illustrator:
Lane Smith**

**Kristy M. Dettman, Grade 4
Whitefish Bay, Wisconsin**

Black Beauty

by Anna Sewell

96 pages

This book made me feel happy and good. Blackie had a happy life, but there were some sad times, too. As I read the book, I felt sad because he wasn't treated well. Some of his owners were mean. I felt good because he had other owners who gave him food and shelter.

I liked the main character, Black Beauty, because he had lots of adventures. Blackie made many new friends. They are Ginger and Merrylegs. Merrylegs is a fat gray pony. He has a thick mane and a tall and very pretty head. Ginger is a chestnut mare. She had mean owners who took her from her mother when she was little and put her with other young colts. She would snap and try to bite a lot.

I learned you can always find happiness even when times are bad. When mean people owned Blackie, he was forced to keep working after he was overtired and not in good shape. No matter how bad things get, they always get better.

By the way, this book is so well written you can really "see" what is happening. I really think you should read this book, whether you like horses or not.

Michelle Primm, Grade 5
Waxhaw, North Carolina

The Secret Notebook
(Kids on the Bus #4)

by Marjorie and Andrew Sharmat

76 pages

The Secret Notebook is a fantastic story in *The Kids on the Bus* series. Marie loses her secret notebook, which contains nasty secrets and Charlie's space-travel report. A few kids on the bus get blamed for taking the notebook. If the notebook is not found, there is going to be a lot of trouble!

I like this book very much because it is like real life but also has a great mystery.

Desiree F. Casado, Grade 4
Actress

Kirsten Learns a Lesson: A School Story

by Janet Shaw

72 pages

ADVENTURE

FRIENDSHIP & FAMILY

MULTICULTURAL

Kirsten Learns a Lesson is about a girl named Kirsten who finds a secret Indian friend named Singing Bird. I like the part when Kirsten and Singing Bird are trading gifts. You'll be surprised when you find out what some of the gifts are. The artwork in this book is very realistic. When Kirsten goes on adventures, she reminds me of myself, because I love adventures. I love books about Kirsten, and there is a whole series of her books. If you want to know what happens to Kirsten and Singing Bird, read this book and you'll never want to put it down.

**Melissa Camara, Grade 4
Wayne, New Jersey**

Top Five Ways to Find a Good Book

5. Read book review.
4. Read over someone's shoulder. (But don't let him or her catch you!)
3. Check out the award winners at the library or bookstore.
2. Ask a friend, parent, librarian, or teacher.
1. Read this book!

Meet Kirsten: An American Girl

by Janet Shaw

72 pages

ADVENTURE

CHALLENGE/ COURAGE

FRIENDSHIP & FAMILY

In the summer of 1854, after a long and dangerous journey on a small ship, Kirsten Larson and her family arrive in America. Everything in the new land is different from the small village Kirsten left behind in Sweden. The way people dress, how they talk, and the ways they travel are all strange to her. Will she ever feel at home in this new place? Getting lost in a big city and parting with her best friend makes her wonder. It is only when the Larsons arrive at a tiny farm on the edge of the frontier that Kirsten believes Papa's promise that America will be a land filled with happy opportunity for all of them. I personally think that this is an interesting book, and I recommend it to all.

**Maryann Papasodero, Grade 4
Mahopac, New York**

The Giving Tree

by Shel Silverstein

56 pages

ADVENTURE

FANTASY & FOLKLORE

FRIENDSHIP & FAMILY

This book by Shel Silverstein is unforgettable. The story is about a tree and a boy, and how they loved each other. The boy would play games with the tree. As he grew older, he wanted things from the tree. The tree gave what she had, such as her apples, then her branches, and finally her trunk.

The drawings are simple, yet they helped tell the story. People of all ages will enjoy this book.

The tree in this book is loving and giving. The boy is selfish and uncaring. I wish people would be more like the tree in this story.

Ashley Ahlers, Grade 4
Mahopac, New York

A Light in the Attic

by Shel Silverstein

176 pages

ADVENTURE

POETRY

I think the best book in the world is *A Light in the Attic* by Shel Silverstein. Here are some AWESOME poems to look up and read: "Moon-Catchin' Net," "Stop Thief!," and MY favorite, "Kidnapped!" I rate these three poems the best in the book. If you want to get the full effect of this book, I suggest you climb a tree and read it!

Brad Bringal, Grade 6
Oak Forest, Illinois

Author: Shel Silverstein

Author! Author!

Shel Silverstein, an award-winning creator of both books and music, claims that he began writing only after failing at baseball, his first love. He is happy with the way things turned out, though. He says, "You can go crazy with some of the wonderful stuff there is in life."

Where the Sidewalk Ends

by Shel Silverstein

Where the Sidewalk Ends is a funny poetry book by Shel Silverstein. The poems have characters such as Sarah Cynthia Sylvia Stout and Lazy Jane. The pictures are really funny. My favorite poem was "Listen to the Mustn'ts." Not everyone will like it, but everyone should give it a try.

I recommend this book to anyone who has a sense of humor and a preference for poetry. You also have to have an imagination. A book to enjoy and laugh at, it is perfect for Saturday afternoons when you're looking for something to do.

Author: Shel Silverstein

> **Alyson McKay, Grade 6**
> **Anaheim, California**

Storms

by Seymour Simon

I read this really good book called *Storms* and I wanted to tell you about it. It's about how storms develop and how weathermen track them. It even shows how a storm can give birth to a tornado, how tornadoes form, and how fast a tornado's wind speed is.

I liked this book because it showed actual pictures of a tornado's birth. It also gave many fascinating facts about storms, tornadoes, and lightning. That's all I'll say for now. . . except: Why don't you read *Storms* for yourself?

> **Christina Svabic, Grade 6**
> **Stafford, Texas**

It's Not Nice to Fool Mother Nature

Since there's no way to stop a hurricane, scientists are trying to keep them from starting. They've tried things like putting dry ice in the clouds to make it rain before the storm reaches the coast. Their attempts have not been very successful. The safest way to avoid a hurricane is to get away from it.

The Rescuers Down Under

by A. L. Singer

64 pages

The Rescuers Down Under is an exciting book. Bernard and Miss Bianca, the top mouse agents with The Rescue Aid Society, are on their most difficult mission ever. They've been sent to Australia to rescue a boy who has been kidnapped by the evil poacher, Percival McLeach. McLeach wants to find a rare golden eagle, and the boy, Cody, is the only one who knows where it is. Will Bernard and Miss Bianca be able to stop the poacher from carrying out his cruel plans, or will McLeach and his six-foot-long lizard, Joanna, have the last laugh? I recommend this book to people who like adventure stories!!

**Brittany Orpin, Grade 3
Warminster, Pennsylvania**

Idea Factory

Q. Where do writers get their ideas?
A. Everywhere!

Serious writers keep idea files or notebooks. You can, too. Get a pack of 3-by-5 notecards or a notebook small enough to carry with you everywhere. Whenever you come across something interesting—that you've read, thought, overheard, seen—write it down. Immediately!

Waitress

by D. Smith

144 pages

The sound of wailing rose through the silence. Then the wails turned into screams. That awful noise was coming from the ladies' room.

This story is about a teenage girl, Paula, who just moved to a different town. She needs money, so she starts to work as a waitress at the Dog House (a restaurant). That's when all the strange things begin to happen. Paula starts to get threatening phone calls, Coralynn gets burned, and Paula gets locked in the freezer. The main characters involved in the mystery are Paula, Trixie, Coralynn, Cookie, and Garth.

What I really liked about the book is it is suspenseful and kept me on the edge of my seat. I recommend *Waitress* to anyone who likes a good mystery.

**Danielle DiPinto, Grade 6
Somers, Connecticut**

A Taste of Blackberries

by Doris Buchanan Smith

Do you like books that talk about friends and having a good friendship? Well, here's one that you will like, and it's called *A Taste of Blackberries*! It's about two boys who are great friends. The illustrations are wonderful, but as you read the book you can form pictures in your mind, too. As I was reading, I had a taste of blackberries in my mouth. This book touched my heart. I hope it touches your heart, too.

Author: Doris Buchanan Smith

**Joseph Holder, Grade 5
Ozark, Alabama**

Mostly Michael

by Robert Kimmel Smith

This is a story about an eleven-year-old boy who gets a diary for his birthday from his Aunt Helene. He thinks it is the dumbest present in the world, and he is so mad he could spit. He says he has the worst life in the world because his father is always working and he had to do ten book reports during the summer because he turned in the same book report twice. His sister, Mindy, is a pest, and she isn't potty-trained. A girl named Carrie thinks she is Michael's girlfriend, but he keeps on telling her he isn't her boyfriend. My favorite part is when Mindy was lost in the mall and she was in the lost and found taking a sprinkle. I liked this book because it was made like a diary. I think people with a good sense of humor would like this book. I'd rate this book a 9.5. Mike learned a lesson that his life isn't so bad.

**Brandon Purington, Grade 5
Weare, New Hampshire**

The War With Grandpa

by Robert Kimmel Smith

128 pages

The War With Grandpa is a funny and moving book.

I liked the main character in a way, but I also thought he was selfish at times. When Peter's grandpa came, Peter had to give up his room. Even though there were other rooms in the house, Peter's parents chose his room. Peter was very angry. He tried to get his room back by talking to his parents, but that didn't work, so he decided to go to war with his grandpa. Both Peter and his grandpa do a lot of foolish stuff. Peter steals his grandpa's false teeth and his grandpa gets really mad. Then Grandpa gets back at Peter by making him late for school. It is so funny! I like the artwork in this book because it shows what happens, but I wish it was in color.

I recommend this book to anyone who has fought with a family member, anyone who likes funny books, and anyone who thinks this book sounds interesting. I have read this one twice.

Alison Boyd, Grade 4
Port Jefferson, New York

A Whole Lotta Sharin' Goin' On

Peter isn't the only one sharing a home with a grandparent. The U.S. Census Bureau reports that several million American children are living with their grandparents.

Encyclopedia Brown and the Case of the Dead Eagles

by Donald J. Sobol

96 pages

This book is part of a series. I liked the main character because he's a ten-year-old boy who helps kids in Idaville solve mysteries. The people who make the most problems are Bugs Meany and his Tigers, and Wilford Wiggins, a high school dropout who tries to get easy money. I liked this book, but I'd change one thing: I'd change the way the ending is—you have to flip to a different page for the solution of the mystery. I'd like the solution to be right there. This book made me think about how I can help people.

Tony Blasco, Grade 3
Pleasant Hill, Iowa

The Wright Brothers at Kitty Hawk

by Donald J. Sobol

128 pages

ADVENTURE

BIOGRAPHY

CHALLENGE/
COURAGE

HISTORY

In *The Wright Brothers at Kitty Hawk* you will read about two brothers named Orville and Wilbur Wright, who shared a dream of flying. First they tried to fly in a glider, then in an airplane. It took awhile for them to succeed, but they finally did. They had an idea for a plane with motors, and it worked and flew for 59 seconds! I think you should read this book because it teaches you never ever to give up.

**Eric Henne, Grade 5
Weathersfield, Connecticut**

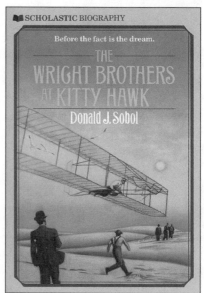

If You Want to Scare Yourself

by Angela Sommer-Bodenburg

112 pages

THRILLS &
CHILLS

This book is about a boy who has injured his leg. He is bored and has nothing to do. He bugs everyone until they tell him scary stories. Believe me, the five stories he hears will knock your socks off. This is a very good book because it teaches you to use your imagination.

**Heather St. Preux, Grade 5
Brooklyn, New York**

A Writer's Corner

Inspired to write? Make yourself a studio. Include:

1. **Desk and chair.** A clipboard and cushion will do.
2. **Paper.** All sorts, lined and unlined.
3. **Writing instruments.** Pens, pencils, a computer or word processor, if possible.
4. **Office supplies.** Paper clips, stapler, tape, glue stick, stamps, envelopes.
5. **Bulletin board.** Tack up ideas, quotes, pictures, anything to jump-start your creativity!

The Sign of the Beaver

by Elizabeth George Speare

144 pages

ADVENTURE

CHALLENGE/
COURAGE

FRIENDSHIP
& FAMILY

HISTORY

Here is a perfect book to help the reader relive the past. Thirteen-year-old Matt is the main character. He has to stay and guard the family cabin in the woods until his father's return. He was very lonely. One day, a strange man in a ragged army coat comes to the house. He steals Matt's father's rifle. After that, Matt is forced to discover new ways to live in the forest without the use of a rifle. Luckily, he becomes friends with an Indian boy who helps him. This is an exciting story about living in the wilderness in the 1700s. As I read, I felt like I was a character in the story.

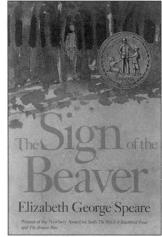

John Perez, Grade 4
East Brunswick, New Jersey

Call It Courage

by Armstrong Sperry

96 pages

ADVENTURE

CHALLENGE/
COURAGE

MULTICULTURAL

Call It Courage is about Mafatu, a ten-year-old Polynesian boy. Mafatu is called a coward by the people of his village because he is afraid of the sea. You see, hen he was a baby, the sea killed his mother. One day, Mafatu can no longer stand all the jokes about his fear, so he sails out to sea in his canoe with only his dog to protect him. When he reaches land, he faces many challenges. Fortunately, he is able to meet these challenges and overcome his fears.

My favorite part in the book is when Mafatu kills the warthog.

This is one of my all-time favorite books. I think you should read this book because it has lots of action, is very well written, and won the Newbery Medal. It makes you realize that you, too, can overcome your fears.

Tim LaVigne, Grade 5
Snyder, New York

171

Maniac Magee

by Jerry Spinelli

192 pages

CHALLENGE/
COURAGE

FRIENDSHIP
& FAMILY

MULTICULTURAL

SPORTS

Maniac Magee is a wonderful story about an eleven-year-old orphan boy, Jeffrey, who is nicknamed Maniac. He lives with his aunt and uncle who hate each other. Maniac decides that is no way to live, so he runs away. Life on the road is one big adventure!

Word on the street is Maniac can run faster than the speed of light, untie any knot, and catch any ball thrown to him. A lot of people rave about the things Maniac can do, but some people hate him. They don't think he should live with his friend Amanda's family.

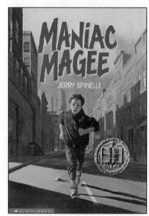

Every kid should read this book because it's about the importance of all different kinds of people learning to live together. I loved this book!

**Thora Birch, Grade 6
Actress**

STAR REVIEW

There's a Girl in My Hammerlock

by Jerry Spinelli

208 pages

CHALLENGE/
COURAGE

SPORTS

There's a Girl in My Hammerlock is a truly exciting book! It is about a girl named Macy who goes out for the wrestling team when she doesn't make the cheerleading squad. Most of the boys from other schools do not want to wrestle her, so they forfeit their matches.

Macy reminds me of myself, because I am always wrestling with my brothers. I like her because she is spunky and doesn't let anyone push her around! If you like books about people participating in unconventional sports, then *There's a Girl in My Hammerlock* is for you!

**Samantha Harvey, Grade 5
Land O'Lakes, Florida**

Author! Author!

Jerry Spinelli, the author of many humorous books for children about growing up, won a Newbery Medal among other awards for *Maniac Magee.* The inspiration to write children's books came from one of his seven kids who was always eating food that Spinelli was saving for himself. The resulting book was called *Space Station Seventh Grade.*

Bad Dreams (Fear Street Series)

by R. L. Stine

176 pages

THRILLS & CHILLS

MYSTERY

This is a very exciting book. In this story, a girl named Maggie moves into a new house and, surprisingly, the owners left an old canopy bed in her room. She decided to keep it even though her sister wanted it. If only she had known the horrifying secret the bed held, she might have answered differently. She sleeps in it every night and every night witnesses the same murder. Every night the same girl beckons to her for help. Then her dreams start coming true. She sees the exact same girl from her dreams. No matter how many R. L. Stine books you have read, you will never suspect the ending of this wonderful, suspenseful, amazing, frightening book!

This is one of the best books I've ever read! I could not put it down. I recommend it if you like R. L. Stine's *Fear Street,* Point books, and/or any other good murder mystery. I absolutely guarantee this book will keep you on the edge of your seat! I think you will have an excellent time reading it! Happy reading!

**Denise Simone, Grade 6
Bronx, New York**

Go Eat Worms! (Goosebumps #21)

by R. L. Stine

144 pages

FRIENDSHIP & FAMILY

THRILLS & CHILLS

MYSTERY

They're creepy and they're crawly—they're totally disgusting! Obsessed with worms? That's putting it mildly. In *Go Eat Worms!*, Todd is so fascinated with worms he keeps a worm farm in his basement! Most of all, Todd loves torturing his sister and her best friend with worms, dropping them down their backs. When he cuts a worm in half, Todd notices something strange. The rest of the worms seem to stare at him. I really enjoyed the strange surprises in this story.

**Maurice Chevalier, Grade 4
Houston, Texas**

Are You My Mother?

Cats give birth to kittens, and dogs give birth to puppies, but do worms give birth to wormlets? Worms come from eggs hatched in soil and grow up by themselves. Even stranger, every earthworm can be a mother and a father, because each one can lay eggs.

The Haunted Mask (Goosebumps #11)

by R. L. Stine

`144 pages`

FRIENDSHIP & FAMILY

THRILLS & CHILLS

MYSTERY

A girl named Carly Beth is mad because her friends are making fun of her for believing in ghosts and witches. To get back at them, she goes to a mask and costume shop to buy a scary mask to frighten her friends on Halloween night. The owner of the shop has a forbidden room blocked with a sheet. In that room, he keeps his "special" masks. Carly Beth looks behind the sheet and sees the mask she has to have. The salesman tells her he is sorry, but those masks are ABSOLUTELY not for sale. Carly Beth pleads with the salesman because her hopes are high about the one mask in the corner. They argue for a long time. Finally he gives in and lets her have the mask. But he warns, "You'll be sorry!" What happened next? Find out for yourself. I highly recommend this *Goosebumps* book to everyone! You won't be able to put it down!

Brian Brozanski, Grade 4
Pittsburgh, Pennsylvania

Indiana Jones and the Cult of the Mummy's Crypt

by R. L. Stine

`117 pages`

ADVENTURE

THRILLS & CHILLS

MYSTERY

Do any of you like interactive books? (An IN-TER-AC-TIVE book is a book that has two-way options for each problem. You decide which one to choose.) Do you like scary books? If you do, be sure to read *Indiana Jones and the Cult of the Mummy's Crypt*. This book is a combination of interactive, adventure, and horror. It is a fun book to read because you can choose what you and Indiana Jones do. Sometimes you make a wrong turn into the room of the . . . TIGERS!!! or get tied up onto a pillar . . . WHEN THE MUMMY'S TOMB CREAKS OPEN!!! You can read it over and over again, but each time something different is waiting to be read, and you read it . . . THE MUMMIES ARE WALKING BY NOW. They leave footprints of ancient dust as they move forward, their rotted arms outstretched. The air smells musty and stale . . . But beware— you have two choices in reading this book . . . LIFE OR DEATH!!!!

Daniel Michaeli, Grade 4
New York, New York

My Hairiest Adventure
(Goosebumps #26)

by R. L. Stine

144 pages

ADVENTURE

FRIENDSHIP & FAMILY

THRILLS & CHILLS

This book is awesome! Larry Boyd is a twelve-year-old who loves dogs but always gets chased by them! One day, before band practice, Larry finds a bottle of "Insta-Tan" lotion. Larry and all his friends decide to put a little on their skin. Then Larry reads the writing on the bottle: DO NOT USE AFTER FEBRUARY, 1991! What Larry and his friends don't know is what that date will mean to them! This was definitely MY hairiest adventure! Read it for yourself!

Andy Barragry, Grade 5
Cedarburg, Wisconsin

What Scares You, Mr. Stine?

When R. L. Stine was very young, he liked *Grimms Fairy Tales* and Norse legends. Later he read ghost stories, joke books, sports books, and science fiction. His biggest goosebumps, however, came from listening to scary stories on the radio!

One Day in Horrorland
(Goosebumps #16)

by R. L. Stine

144 pages

FRIENDSHIP & FAMILY

THRILLS & CHILLS

MYSTERY

This is an awesome adventure story; once you start reading, you can't stop!! It reminded me of Spooky World, a horror park in Massachusetts.

When the Morris family decided to go for a nice quiet day at Zoo Gardens theme park, something just had to go wrong. They took a wrong turn and found another theme park called Horrorland where your nightmares come to life. Lizzy knew in less than one hour they would all be lying in their coffins (and she's the brave one in the family). To start off, the car blew up, on one ride they almost lost their friend, and they got put into a torture chamber. Find out if the Morris family survives or if they become "horror food!!"

I definitely recommend this book, plus other *Goosebumps* books, to anyone who is in for an adventure story and likes a chill running up his or her spine.

Amanda Kraemer, Grade 4
Winchester, Massachusetts

175

One Day in Horrorland
(Goosebumps #16)

by R. L. Stine

`144 pages`

FRIENDSHIP & FAMILY

THRILLS & CHILLS

MYSTERY

How long do you think you would survive in a park full of spooky houses, caves, and mazes? I don't think you would last ten minutes.

In this book, you won't believe the horrible, spooky things that happen to Lizzy, Lake, and Clay on their vacation. First, Clay gets lost on the Slide of Doom. Then, the other two go to look for him and almost get smashed in the House of Mirrors when the walls close in on them. Then, they get locked in a maze full of monsters.

If you want to find out if they make it out, you'll have to check this book out at your local library. If you like scary books by R.L. Stine, you'll like this one.

Richard Allan, Grade 6
Mound City, Missouri

Phantom of the Auditorium
(Goosebumps #24)

by R. L. Stine

`144 pages`

FRIENDSHIP & FAMILY

THRILLS & CHILLS

MYSTERY

This book is about a phantom haunting Woods Mill Middle School. Two kids named Brooke and Zeke are in the school play called "The Phantom." Then their teacher tells them a legend about the school—a legend about the phantom. Strange things start to happen. A note appears: "Stay Away From My Home Sweet Home!" Scenery is destroyed.

If you like thrilling, chilling, spine-tingling, teeth-rattling books, then I recommend that you read this one.

Kimberly Surber, Grade 3
Dix Hills, New York

Author:
R. L. Stine

Author! Author!

R. L. Stine is the hottest author in the country—outselling adult authors Stephen King, John Grisham, and others! There are over 71 million *Goosebumps* books in print. There's just one reader Stine would still like to win over—his son, Matthew. "He still refuses to read my books," Stine complains. You can find out more about *Goosebumps* and the author on these Web sites:

• http://scholastic.com:80/Goose bumps/Books/Books.html

• http://scholastic.com:80/Goose bumps/Stine/Stine-Home.html

Return of the Mummy
(Goosebumps #23)

by R. L. Stine

144 pages

Do you like scary mystery books? I do. That's why I read the *Goosebumps* series. My favorite *Goosebumps* book is *Return of the Mummy*. It takes place in Egypt. Gabe (the main character) is visiting his Uncle Ben (a scientist who studies mummies) and Gabe's cousin, Sari. Gabe finds out some magic words that are supposed to wake mummies from the dead. Gabe doesn't believe in it, but he says the magic words anyway. Then Gabe and Sari start hearing groans in the pyramid. There's no way those dumb words can wake the dead, or can they?

I like the *Goosebumps* series because R. L. Stine really knows how to keep the suspense and scare you badly.

**Tom Knight, Grade 5
Appleton, Wisconsin**

Rookie of the Year

by Todd Strasser

96 pages

Rookie of the Year is about a boy named Henry who breaks his arm. When he gets his cast off, he discovers that his arm is like a ball launcher! I liked when the Cub players get surprised when an eleven-year-old boy (Henry) joined them. It feels unbelievable that an eleven-year-old boy could get into a professional baseball team. I recommend this book to everybody who likes baseball.

**Angel S. Bontilao, Grade 4
Jacksonville, Florida**

Don't Try This at Home!

Rookie of the Year, about a young boy good enough to play professional baseball, is only fantasy. Baseball coaches warn children: Don't throw harder than your strength allows. It will hurt your throw and maybe even your arm. You will get stronger as you get older.

The Nutcracker: A Story and a Ballet

by Ellen Switzer

112 pages

This is a fabulous story. It is about a girl named Marie who lives in Germany. Her family is having a Christmas party. Suddenly, Marie's godfather comes and gives her a nutcracker doll. That night, after the party, everything starts to grow big and come to life. A pack of giant mice attack Marie and her nutcracker doll, which is now alive and taller than she is!

Later, the nutcracker turns into a handsome prince. He and Marie go to an enchanted land called the Sweets. Marie and the nutcracker prince are served candy and entertained with dances. *The Nutcracker* is a romantic and artistically written book that I think you will really like.

Samantha Lipman, Grade 5
Toledo, Ohio

Check It Out!

The Nutcracker was originally performed as a ballet in Russia in 1892 with music written by the famous composer Peter Ilich Tchaikovsky. It is still performed today by ballet companies around the world. Look for this holiday treat this winter.

Let the Circle Be Unbroken

by Mildred D. Taylor

432 pages

"We sped through the darkness. . . . Stones hit noisily against the car's underbelly and dust swirled around us as the lights cast an eerie glow, making the trees loom larger than they were." That is just a sample of the wonderful imagery Mildred D. Taylor gives in this book, sequel to *Roll of Thunder, Hear My Cry.* Her gripping imagery makes the book very easy to understand and relate to. As she explains the main character, Cassie, I found myself relating to her and understanding how she felt. This is a powerful feeling and makes the book enjoyable to read.

This book is about a black family, the Logans, living in Mississippi at a very rough time, in 1935. It explains how white people treated black families and how poorly paid they were for doing hard work. Just because of the color of their skin, they had trouble finding work. Ms. Taylor tells about things that many people denied for quite a while.

Ms. Taylor's theme was quite obvious: Having a family is better than anything, and with them you can accomplish anything, no matter what. This book shows how prejudiced people can be. People who like history will not be able to put this book down.

Megan Rhoten, Grade 5
Hampstead, Missouri

Roll of Thunder, Hear My Cry

by Mildred D. Taylor

276 pages

CHALLENGE/ COURAGE

DRAMA

FRIENDSHIP & FAMILY

MULTICULTURAL

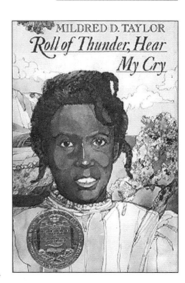

I've just finished the best book I've ever read! *Roll of Thunder, Hear My Cry* by Mildred Taylor is about a black girl named Cassie and her family who are going through terrible hardships trying to cope with racism in the South in 1933.

The family's land means everything to them. They have a lot of pride, because they know they worked hard for their achievements and no one could take that away from them. Read about how determined the Logan family is to solve their problem and overcome racism.

I like how loving the Logan family is. If you read this book, you'll understand that if you should come to a sudden upheaval in life, never give up and always try your best.

**Evelyn Stansberry, Grade 6
Chicago, Illinois**

And the Winner Is...

Roll of Thunder, Hear My Cry won the Newbery Medal in 1977. Every year, only one author wins the award for making the "most distinguished contribution" to American children's literature. The medal is named after John Newbery, the first Englishman to print and sell children's books.

The Terrible Turnoff and Me

by Joan Thompson

160 pages

FRIENDSHIP & FAMILY

HUMOR

Could you imagine living without TV for a whole month?! Well, if you can't—try reading *The Terrible Turnoff and Me* by Joan Thompson. It has 160 pages, but in those short pages a lot sure happens! It's about Susan Hubbard, Ray, her brother, Joey, and a lot of other kids. They were picked for a school project to either turn off their TV completely, or watch four hours a day. You'll be surprised what Susan and Ray discover by turning off their TV. If you like that, try *The Mudpak and Me,* also by Joan Thompson. Now turn off the TV and read this book!

**Alyson Dusseault, Grade 5
Swampscott, Massachusetts**

The Hobbit

by J. R. R. Tolkien

320 pages

ADVENTURE

FANTASY & FOLKLORE

HUMOR

What's a hobbit? A hobbit is a little fat being that lives in a hole and is shorter than a dwarf. This book is about a hobbit named Bilbo Baggins who goes on an adventure as a "thief." The story starts off when a wizard named Gandalf meets the hobbit Bilbo. He takes Bilbo through dangerous forests, fighting dragons, and meeting strange people, all for the sake of a treasure. This journey guarantees to leave you bewildered and surprised. Especially since hobbits hate adventures!

This book will not only entertain you but will make you laugh. The characters say funny things, like when Gollum says, "Precious, precious, he took our precious," referring to a magic ring. This line may not seem funny, but put together with the rest of the page it will make you crack a smile.

Check It Out!

The Hobbit is Tolkien's best-known work, but if you want something that's a little shorter (80 pages), check out *Farmer Giles of Ham.* It's also a Tolkienian fantasy tale, taking place long ago in a middle kingdom of Britain. After Farmer Giles scares off a wandering giant (almost accidentally), everyone expects him to dispatch just as easily the destructive dragon Chrysophylax Dives.

If you want to learn more about hobbits, and you like adventure books filled with magic, sword fighting, and good vs. evil, this book is for you!

Brandon Kreines, Grade 5
Cincinnati, Ohio

Cajun Night Before Christmas

by "Trosclair"

48 pages

FANTASY & FOLKLORE

HUMOR

MULTICULTURAL

If you want a new twist to *The Night Before Christmas,* then read *Cajun Night Before Christmas*. This Santa has eight alligators who pull his skiff on the bayou to everyone's house. This story is written in Cajun language like this:

> To de top o' de porch
> To de top o' de wall
> Make crawl, alligator,
> An be sho' you don' fall.

My favorite part of the book is when Santa sits on "dem red hot coal." The pictures in this book are really funny, too! I bet you'll like this book any time of the year.

Kirk Perschbacher, Grade 4
Oscoda, Michigan

The Adventures of Tom Sawyer

by Mark Twain

228 pages

ADVENTURE

CHALLENGE/ COURAGE

FRIENDSHIP & FAMILY

HUMOR

Do you like adventure, scariness, sadness, and happiness? If you do, here's the book for you. It is called *The Adeventures of Tom Sawyer*. The author is Mark Twain. It's about a little boy who loves getting into trouble. There is a murder in a graveyard, then a search for buried treasure, and a narrow escape from death! Join Tom Sawyer and his friends as they fill every minute of their time with wild adventures: forming secret societies, discovering girls, attending their own funerals, solving a mystery, and becoming heroes. I really liked this classic story, and I have a hunch you will, too!

**Kelly Caudle, Grade 4
Kenner, Louisiana**

Author! Author!

Mark Twain is one of America's most famous authors. But before he wrote novels, he did lots of other things—like being a riverboat pilot on the Mississippi! That's why steamboats and life along the great Mississippi River are featured in several of his books, including *The Adventures of Huckleberry Finn* and *Life on the Mississippi*.

The Prince and the Pauper

by Mark Twain

228 pages

ADVENTURE

CHALLENGE/ COURAGE

FRIENDSHIP & FAMILY

This book is about a prince and a pauper who were born on the same day. The prince met the pauper when the palace guards threw the pauper out. The prince said, "Stop." He invited the pauper in. The prince wanted to know what the pauper's life was like. So they changed clothes and took each other's places.

I recommend this book because it's an adventure. Mark Twain wrote a lot of books, but I think this was his best of all.

**Patrick Cunniff, Grade 4
Medford, Massachusetts**

Gift Horse (Animal Inn #12)

by Virginia Vail

128 pages

ANIMAL

CHALLENGE/ COURAGE

DRAMA

FRIENDSHIP & FAMILY

This story takes place in Pennsylvania at the Animal Inn. Valentine is the main character. She likes to be called Val. Val loves animals. She likes horses the most. She cares a lot about her horse, the Ghost. Toby is Val's best friend at the Animal Inn. They both work there. Val's dad, Doc, is the doctor at the Animal Inn. His wife died awhile ago. Now he has a girlfriend named Catherine. This book is full of decision making.

The Ghost is Val's horse. He has cataracts in his eyes. Val has saved up over $1,000 to have him operated on. Val tells her dad what she wants to do. He tells her that there is only a small chance that the operation will work. If the operation does not work, the Ghost will be totally blind. Val is not sure if she wants to have it done or not. Will the Ghost get the operation? To find out, read this great book!

I like this book a lot because it's about animals and decision making. It is also very happy. I recommend this book to others. I would love to read other books by this author.

Trista R. Rink, Grade 5
Lansing, Michigan

Jumanji

by Chris Van Allsburg

32 pages

ADVENTURE

FANTASY & FOLKLORE

FRIENDSHIP & FAMILY

THRILLS & CHILLS

I just read a cool book called *Jumanji*. It was written and illustrated by Chris Van Allsburg. The book is about two kids who find a game under a tree. When the parents go out, they start to play the game. When they roll the dice, whatever they land on really happens. For example, when they roll a 7, the space they land on says, "Lion attacks, move back 2 spaces." They turn around to see a big lion about to pounce on them. But in the instructions it says, once the game of Jumanji has started, it won't be over until one player reaches the golden city. This means they can't stop playing until they finish the game. All kinds of crazy and horrible things happen.

The artwork in the book is realistic, but I wish it was in color instead of black and white. But overall, I liked the book a lot because it is funny and scary.

Tess Barbato, Grade 4
Port Jefferson, New York

The Polar Express

by Chris Van Allsburg

32 pages

ADVENTURE

FANTASY & FOLKLORE

FRIENDSHIP & FAMILY

This wonderful story takes place on Christmas Eve. It's about a boy who is waiting to hear the jingling bells of Santa's sleigh. But instead of Santa's sleigh, he hears the sound of a train. Then he goes outside and decides to get on the train. Where will the train go? What will happen next? Once you start reading this book, you won't be able to put it down. Not only is the story great, but the illustrations are absolutely terrific!! I recommend this book to anyone who enjoys the holidays and good books.

Rajir Jayadevan, Grade 3
Port Jefferson, New York

What If?

Most of Chris Van Allsburg's stories begin as pictures in his mind. He asks himself, "What if?" and "What then?" *The Polar Express* grew from a mental image of a boy who sees a train stopped in front of his house. What if you tried to create a book this way? What then?

The Polar Express

by Chris Van Allsburg

32 pages

ADVENTURE

FANTASY & FOLKLORE

FRIENDSHIP & FAMILY

The Polar Express is about a boy who didn't know if Santa Claus was real. One night, a train brought the boy and some other children to the North Pole. Santa Claus told the boy he could have any gift he wanted. He asked for a bell, which Santa gave him. On the way home, the bell was lost. On Christmas morning, the bell was under the Christmas tree, but only the people who believed in Santa could hear it.

I really liked *The Polar Express* because it is about the spirit of Christmas. I also liked the author's choice of words. The story seemed to come alive. The illustrations are very lifelike and colorful. This book will be enjoyed by people of all ages.

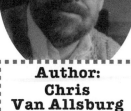

Author: Chris Van Allsburg

Michael Stevens, Grade 4
Whitesboro, New York

The Wreck of the Zephyr

by Chris Van Allsburg

32 pages

ADVENTURE

CHALLENGE/ COURAGE

FANTASY & FOLKLORE

A boat can fly? If you read this book, you'll meet a man who tells a tale about flying boats. One of the boats is called the *Zephyr*. It's a fascinating tale for children of all ages. It's about a boy who thinks he's the best sailor of all time. He heads out toward the open sea on a stormy day, when suddenly a gust of wind blows the boom around and it hits him on the head. Later he wakes up and finds himself in a land where boats can fly.

I liked the book because it involved magic. After I read the book, I felt like flying the *Zephy*. I wish that something like that would happen to me!

If you have enjoyed other books like *The Polar Express* and *Jumanji,* you'll enjoy this one. Van Allsburg's beautifully detailed artwork and story are fun to read!

**Conrad Bower, Grade 5
Cincinnati, Ohio**

A Journey to the Centre of the Earth

by Jules Verne

64 pages

ADVENTURE

CHALLENGE/ COURAGE

SCIENCE FICTION

This book taught me that nothing is impossible. I know it's a fantasy story, but it was so real that really I believed it.

There are three main characters: Professor Hardwigg, his nephew, Harry, and their guide, Hans. Hans is my favorite because he's the one who takes them to the center of the earth. In one scene they run out of water, and so Hans goes out to look for some. He hears something—water! Unfortunately it's covered by a rock wall, so Hans takes a crowbar and hits it. Finally water comes gushing out! That was cool.

This book made me realize there is always something left to accomplish. The challenge is out there, so never think there's nothing new to try. Believe me there is!

**Kevin Kachar, Grade 4
Racine, Wisconsin**

Fiction That's Scientific

Science fiction is fairly new. When *A Journey to the Centre of the Earth* came out in 1864, nobody called it sci-fi. But French author Jules Verne is considered a main creator of the genre, because his stories, while unbelievably fantastic, are also "so real," as our reviewer points out. That's because Verne based all of the scientific elements on scientific fact.

The Ice Princess

by Nicholas Walker

128 pages

The Ice Princess by Nicholas Walker is a great book to read. It is about two friends who are ice-skating partners. Their names are Samantha and Alex. Samantha and Alex finally have the chance to go for the gold. But Samantha hasn't been feeling so well and her parents think that the ice-dancing competition may have something to do with it. They want to send her to a creepy old boarding school until she recovers.

But Samantha and Alex are still determined to win the championship, even though the world seems to be against them. If everything goes as planned, they have a chance at winning. But if something goes wrong, Samantha may never skate again! I would recommend this book to friends. I read it over and over, and still want to read it again.

Catherine Thangathurai, Grade 5 ··········
Los Angeles, California

Pride of Puerto Rico:
The Life of Roberto Clemente

by Paul R. Walker

132 pages

This book is about Roberto Clemente, a great baseball player and a great person. He died in a plane crash while flying to help earthquake victims in Nicaragua. He isn't the Home Run King, but he will be remembered by millions.

Roberto and I are alike because we both love baseball. It would have been a dream come true to have played ball with him.

Sean Cox, Grade 5
Iola, Kansas

From Puerto Rico to Pittsburgh

The great Roberto Clemente played right field for the Pittsburgh Pirates and was known for his tremendous talent in fielding, throwing, and hitting. He helped the Pirates win two World Series, in 1960 and 1971, and was named outstanding player of the 1971 series. Soon after, he hit his 3,000th hit. Read the book to learn more.

Ferret in the Bedroom, Lizards in the Fridge

by Bill Wallace

144 pages

ANIMAL

FRIENDSHIP & FAMILY

HUMOR

Ferret in the Bedroom, Lizards in the Fridge by Bill Wallace is about a girl named Liz. Her father is a zoologist. There are animals every-where! It is funny when Ivan, their pet ibex, is chasing all of Liz's friends in their backyard. How would you like digging in your freezer and pulling out a frozen lizard! Liz's friends don't like all the animals, and Liz and her father get into a fight. Then her father takes all the animals to work. The story makes me think about true friendship and making choices. I recommend this book to people who like funny books or animals.

Laura Brigham, Grade 3
Depew, New York

Two Old Women: An Alaska Legend of Betrayal, Courage and Survival

by Velma Wallis

160 pages

CHALLENGE/ COURAGE

DRAMA

ENVIRONMENT

MULTICULTURAL

Here's a book about how two complaining women survived near the Arctic Circle. It starts like this: Ch'idzgyaak and Sa are the oldest in their Inuit Tribe. Their tribe is running out of food because there are not enough animals to hunt. One morning, the chief of the tribe calls a meeting and says that they will have to leave Sa and Ch'idzgyaak behind. The chief believes they are too old and will cause problems and make the tribe go slowly. When the rest of the tribe leaves quietly, the two old women sit before the fire for a moment. Sa soon brakes the silence. She said this: "If we are going to die, let's die trying." If you want to know if they survived or not, read *Two Old Women*. I did. And it was well worth it.

Chong Moua, Grade 4
Lompoc, California

Justin and the Best Biscuits in the World

by Mildred Pitts Walter

128 pages

CHALLENGE/COURAGE

FRIENDSHIP & FAMILY

HISTORY

MULTICULTURAL

This book is about a ten-year-old boy whose grandfather is a cowboy. It was fun to read because Justin has two sisters who boss him around just like my sisters boss me. I know how he feels when everybody is on his case and always telling him what to do. Justin's sisters said he could not do anything right. But Grandfather took him to his ranch and showed him how to clean his room, cook, and take care of himself. Now he can do something his sisters can't do: He can make the best biscuits in the world.

I recommend this book to all people. This book will make you feel good.

**Brian White, Grade 5
Chicago, Illinois**

Black Cowboys

In this book, Justin's grandfather doesn't just teach Justin about baking biscuits. He teaches him quite a few things about American history. For instance, Justin hears about the many African-American cowboys who roped and rode in the Old West—legendary men like Bill Pickett, Jessie Stahl, and Nat Love.

The Camp-Out Mystery
(Boxcar Children #27)

by Gertrude Chandler Warner

192 pages

ADVENTURE

FRIENDSHIP & FAMILY

MYSTERY

The Boxcar Children is a series about a family of children whose parents have died. They live in a boxcar of an old deserted freight train.

The Camp-Out Mystery is about when Henry, Jessie, Violet, Benny, and their grandfather go camping. But when they try to go to sleep, they hear mysterious noises. They even find a note attached to a tree that's pinned by an arrow. Other exciting things happen to them as well, but I don't want to give away the ending. You'll have to read the book yourself to find out who's doing the mysterious things.

Although this is not my favorite Boxcar book, I enjoyed it. I recommend the other books in the series, too, like *The Mystery on the Ice, The Deserted Library Mystery,* and *The Boxcar Children #1.* I like them because they are exciting and you never know what is going to happen.

**Amanda Rote, Grade 4
Oreland, Pennsylvania**

The Ghost Ship Mystery
(Boxcar Children #39)

by Gertrude Chandler Warner

128 pages

ADVENTURE

FRIENDSHIP & FAMILY

MYSTERY

This story is about four children who learn a legend about a ghost ship. It takes place in an old fishing village. When Jessie, Violet, Henry, and Benny get there, they are in for a really good mystery about a ghost ship. The ghost ship comes only on dark and stormy nights. But after a few nights there, they find out just about anything can happen.

In this book I like Benny Alden (that's his last name) because he asks so many questions. Also, I learned that just about anything can happen. If you like spooky mysteries, you should read this book!

Katie Giese, Grade 5
Medford, Wisconsin

The Pizza Mystery
(Boxcar Children #33)

by Gertrude Chandler Warner

128 pages

ADVENTURE

FRIENDSHIP & FAMILY

MYSTERY

If you like mystery books, try *The Pizza Mystery*. It's about four brothers and sisters who are like detectives. They have to find out who is trying to shut down Piccolo's Pizzeria, a restaurant where the children are working for the summer. I think I'm like the Boxcar Children because I like trying to solve problems. Everyone should read this book! It's so interesting that you won't be able to stop reading it until you've finished the whole thing.

Heather George, Grade 5
Denton, Texas

THE PIZZA MYSTERY
created by
GERTRUDE CHANDLER WARNER

Up From Slavery

by Booker T. Washington

BIOGRAPHY

CHALLENGE/COURAGE

HISTORY

The autobiography written by Booker T. Washington entitled *Up From Slavery* is beautifully written.

I felt very sorry for Booker because he was a slave. Then, when he was in debt, he had to travel everywhere to get contributions to pay it off. I liked Booker because he always kept trying to provide things for other people.

This book gave some interesting facts about slavery. I never knew that all a slave got for meals was cornmeal and water. Who would have guessed that slaves had meetings even though they weren't supposed to? It also taught me to keep trying for anything I need.

Booker reminds me of my sister. Even though my sister doesn't always try for others, they both never give up.

This book is so wonderfully written, I recommend it to anyone who likes a good book.

**Jacob Reed, Grade 5
Bryan, Ohio**

Author! Author!

Booker Taliaferro Washington recommended hard work, thrift, and self-help. He followed his own advice. The son of a slave, he graduated from college, founded the Tuskegee Institute in Alabama, and became a spokesman for African Americans. To start Tuskegee, he bought land, built a brick-making kiln—and then made bricks to build classrooms, dormitories, and a chapel!

The Story of the White House

by Kate Waters

HISTORY

The Story of the White House is a great book! You should read it! It shows you everything in the White House. When you read this book, you will find out how many rooms are in the White House and how many phone calls they get a day. You will learn also how many people visit the White House a day. I liked the book because you can learn about the White House. I recommend this book to anybody who wants to learn about where the presidents live.

**Samantha Manzi,
Grade 3
Suffern, New York**

Meet You in the Alley, Mr. President

Every president leaves his mark at the White House—some small and personal, others involving major construction. President Clinton had a track built so that he could continue to jog. President Nixon had a bowling alley put in! The White House also boasts tennis courts and a movie theater.

Ghost Hotel

by Larry Weinberg

160 pages

Ghost Hotel by Larry Weinberg is super-spooky! It's about a girl who is adopted and wants to find her real parents. When her family checks into a hotel, she meets a ghost. And guess what: Anna looks just like the ghost's daughter, who died over 100 years ago. Now she has to travel back in time to find her real parents.

I liked the main character because she is very adventurous. She was determined to find out who her real parents were, and she never gave up. If I could change one thing about the book, I would choose for Anna not to be adopted but to have mean parents instead. Then she could be searching for some adoptive parents who are nice. That would be an interesting twist, don't you think?

Rob Baquet, Grade 5
Port Jefferson, New York

The Adventures of Ratman

by Ellen Weiss and Mel Friedman

64 pages

This book is about a boy named Tod who reads a comic book. At the end of the comic book he finds a form. He fills out the form and sends it in the mail. The next day he gets a box. Inside the box is a rat suit with directions that say "put it on." What happens next? If you want to know, read *Ratman!*

I recommend this book to anyone who likes superheroes.

Lindsay Kahn, Grade 3
Port Jefferson, New York

Storytelling

Want to make a story you love come alive? Try telling it! To get started:

1. **Choose the right story.** Fairy tales, fables, and your own stories are good.
2. **Dramatize.** Use sound effects, "voices," gestures, props.
3. **Rehearse.** Use a mirror, tape recorder, and practice audiences.
4. **Start telling!** For more help, read *The Storyteller's Start-up Book* by Margaret Read MacDonald.

Dinosaur Discoveries: How to Create Your Own Prehistoric World

by Robin West

72 pages

This book is about making dinosaurs out of paper. It shows how to make just about every dinosaur you can think of and create your own prehistoric world.

I like this book not just because it's fun and interesting, but the pictures are good too. I also really like how the author gave the dinosaurs strange names that might not be the same as the ones you are used to hearing. Some of the names are Roberta Rhamphorhynchus, Dimitri Dimetrodon, and Stanley Stegosaurus!

Danny Harris, Grade 3
Bartlett, Illinois

Charlotte's Web

by E. B. White

192 pages

I really liked the book *Charlotte's Web*. It's about a pig named Wilbur who is going to be killed. His friend Charlotte, a spider, tries to save him. There's also a little girl, Fern, who doesn't want the pig to die because her father gave Wilbur to her when he was just a piglet.

I liked how even though the pig was bigger than the spider, the spider was saving the pig's life. You should read this book because it's exciting and you never know what Charlotte's going to plan next.

Angela Wu, Grade 4
Fresh Meadows, New York

"Where's Papa Going With That Ax?"

E. B. White wrote this intriguing first line (and the rest of *Charlotte's Web*) in a boathouse on his farm in Maine. He had a typewriter, a table and bench, a sketch of the Zuckerman farm—and nothing else. A nature lover his whole life, White did careful research on the habits of all the animals in the book.

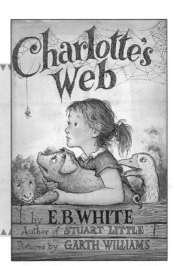

Stuart Little

by E. B. White

ADVENTURE

ANIMAL

FANTASY & FOLKLORE

FRIENDSHIP & FAMILY

When I read *Stuart Little,* I thought a lot about what it would feel like to be a little mouse and live with a family of humans who are, unfortunately, a whole lot bigger than a you!

In the book, Stuart Little goes through a lot of very unusual, but fascinating, adventures, like one part where he had to go down the drain to get his mother's ring. I especially liked the little clothes that were made for him. Well, I won't tell you anything else because I really want you to read this book!!

Jill Rosalie Johnson, Grade 5
Glenrock, Wyoming

Author! Author!

Elwyn Brooks White dreamed up Stuart Little. Really—the humanlike mouse first appeared to him in a dream! White made Stuart the hero of stories he told to his nieces and nephews. When his son Joel loved the stories, too, he decided to write them down.

Author: E. B. White

The Trumpet of the Swan

by E. B. White

ADVENTURE

ANIMAL

FANTASY & FOLKLORE

FRIENDSHIP & FAMILY

Would you like to read about a swan who carries a moneybag, medal, chalkboard, chalk, and a trumpet on his neck? Then *The Trumpet of the Swan* is just the book for you! It is about the unpredictable adventures of Louis, a swan who was well known for his peculiar talents. But none of Louis's fans know the truth about his disability—except a fourth-grader named Sam.

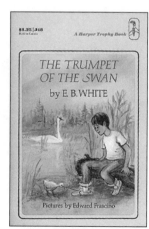

Have fun traveling with Louis through his incredible adventures, and you'll discover what remarkable things this special swan can do! This book deserves to be on everyone's bookshelf.

Sarah Yin, Grade 3
Philadelphia, Pennsylvania

June 29, 1999

by David Wiesner

32 pages

June 29, 1999 is fantastic. It's about Holly Evans who begins to notice really weird things. Here's an example: Giant vegetables start falling out of the sky. But why?

The pictures are great. They are really funny. I would recommend this book to everybody with a sense of humor.

It also gave me something to think about. What is "arugula"?

Mike Stone, Grade 5
Tucson, Arizona

A-WHAT-U-LA?!

Mike Stone, reviewer of *June 29, 1999* asks, "What is arugula?" Arugula is a salad green. Some people think it tastes too bitter, but others like it in soups, salads, and sautéed vegetable dishes. And, Mike, it's good for you, too!

Farmer Boy

by Laura Ingalls Wilder

372 pages

Farmer Boy is about a boy, Almanzo Wilder, growing up on a farm, just like I am. In this book, he plants, harrows, and harvests. He helps his dad in the field, just like I do.

Almanzo has a pet pig named Lucy. He loves horses, but his father won't let him go near them. Instead, Almanzo's father gives him a pair of young oxen to train to pull a sled or a cart.

Almanzo grew up when traditional technology was used instead of the tractors that we use nowadays. But we are still both farm boys, and that's why it is my favorite book of all time.

Jeff Sloan, Grade 6
Everest, Kansas

Illustrator! Illustrator!

Garth Williams worked on the *Little House* books for six years. He met Laura Ingalls Wilder and visited all but one of the houses. He also researched as many details as possible. His illustrations are well loved. But he almost didn't take the job! He didn't think he was good at drawing people.

Little House in the Big Woods

by Laura Ingalls Wilder

Little House in the Big Woods is written by Laura Ingalls Wilder. It is about Laura Ingalls Wilder as a child and how she lived with her family. She lived about 100 years ago. I liked this book because it made me feel like I was really there. This book reminds me of my mother when she tells me about her life as a child. I liked Laura because she was always happy. I recommend this book to kids who like true stories from the past.

Jamie Cherry, Grade 4
Kenner, Louisiana

A Late Start to a Big Success

Laura Ingalls Wilder's books describe her pioneer life from 1870 to 1894. But she didn't write the first book until 1932, when she was 65! Her daughter, Rose Wilder Lane, helped her shape childhood memories into exciting stories, spiced with details of everyday homesteading life. For a different true account of a pioneer girlhood, try *Caddie Woodlawn* and its sequel *Magical Melons* by Carol Ryrie Brink.

Little House on the Prairie

by Laura Ingalls Wilder

This is a fabulous true tale! In this book, Ma, Pa, Laura, Mary, and baby Carrie Ingalls travel in a covered wagon to Indian Country. It took about four weeks. Pa wanted to move from Big Woods because there were too many people living there.

When they got to Indian country, Pa cut some trees and started making a house. The family slept in the wagon until the house was ready. One problem they had was the wolves. One night, the wolves made a circle around the house. Mary and Laura were worried. Laura couldn't sleep. Pa kept looking out the window holes with his gun in one hand until the wolves left.

If I were Laura, I would think life was hard but fun. It sure is nice to have stores and homes closer together than what the Ingallses had. This is one of the best books I have ever read.

Sarah Widman, Grade 5
Sandusky, Ohio

I'll Always Love You

by Hans Wilhelm

32 pages

ANIMAL

FRIENDSHIP & FAMILY

If you have ever had a pet you really loved, you will want to read *I'll Always Love You*. The boy in this story grew up with his dog, Elfie. As Elfie grew older, it didn't matter to the boy that Elfie couldn't do all the things she used to do. He helped Elfie keep up with him. The boy carried "old" Elfie up the stairs every night so they could sleep together like they always did.

This story taught me that it's very important to say, "I'll always love you." It makes everyone feel better just hearing it. Read this book and you'll remember to say, "I'll always love you," to someone you love.

**Michael Laski, Grade 3
Kenmore, New York**

Author:
Hans Wilhelm

The Battle for the Castle

by Elizabeth Winthrop

160 pages

ADVENTURE

FANTASY & FOLKLORE

The best book I read this year was *The Battle for the Castle*. It is a great story about a boy named William who enters a magical world through a toy castle in his attic. The world he visits has a good knight, squires, soldiers—even a cat that used to be a dragon. William battles an army of rats and learns a lot about himself before his visit is over. This book has everything! Action, adventure, and even a lesson!

Bruce Vail, Grade 5
Dunwoody, Georgia

Shadow of a Bull

by Maia Wojciechowska

CHALLENGE/ COURAGE

DRAMA

FRIENDSHIP & FAMILY

MULTICULTURAL

I've just got to tell you about this book I read. It's called *Shadow of a Bull* by Maia Wojciechowska.

This is an excellent book about a boy named Manolo Olivar, who has the difficult task of following in his famous father's footsteps. His peers expect him to be a bullfighter, like his father. The expectations are far too much for him to handle. Read the book to see how he overcomes his problems.

Shadow of a Bull is a Newbery Medal winner.

STAR REVIEW

Shaun Weiss, Grade 8 Actress

176 pages

Bullfight School

Matador-wannabees usually begin training around age twelve. They learn how to lure the bull to charge with a *muleta,* or circular red cloth, using different maneuvers. They also learn how to kill the bull with a sword. Not surprisingly, most trainees give up after getting gored.

George Washington's Socks

by Elvira Woodruff

176 pages

ADVENTURE

FANTASY & FOLKLORE

FRIENDSHIP & FAMILY

HISTORY

George Washington's Socks by Elvira Woodruff is amazing historical fiction. It involves a group of children going back in time to the battle at Trenton during the Revolution.

On their journey, Matthew, Quentin, Hooter, Tony, and Katie see the realities of war—there was no good or bad guy, no right or wrong side, just some soldiers being true to their country. If you like adventure stories, you'll love this book!

Sophia Ortega, Grade 5 Frederick, Colorado

The Swiss Family Robinson

by Johann David Wyss

296 pages

ADVENTURE

CHALLENGE/ COURAGE

FRIENDSHIP & FAMILY

The Swiss Family Robinson is a timeless classic. It shows the hardships a Swiss family has to face when their ship's crew abandons them to survive on their own. The family spots land and ties washtubs together and sails to land. This land is inhabited by humans but is ruled by vicious animals, such as cheetahs, and the treacherous water surrounding the island is home to killer whales and hammerhead sharks! That's all you need to know about this book to get you interested. If you're a go-getter for novels filled with adventure, then you won't be able to put this one down!

Doug Thomas, Grade 6
Sedalia, Missouri

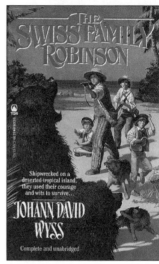

Owl Moon

by Jane Yolen

32 pages

ANIMAL

ENVIRONMENT

FRIENDSHIP & FAMILY

A boy goes owling with his pa. I like this book because I like owls. The illustrations are great, especially the shadows from the trees. I think you should buy *Owl Moon* and read it right now.

Vicky Riggieri, Grade 2
Port Jefferson, New York

Author: Jane Yolen

Whoo, How?

Thanks to special wing feathers, shy owls fly absolutely silently. They can locate sounds precisely because one ear is slightly higher than the other. They also see 10 to 100 times better than people in dim light. Want to see an owl? Hunt like one—search *quietly* at dusk near the woods, watch (with binoculars), and listen carefully.

Secrets in the Attic

by Carol Beach York

112 pages

This scary story is about a girl named Jodie. Jodie lives with her mom and three-year-old brother, Peter, in a small town. Her father was killed in a car accident along with her Uncle Phillip. After the accident, nothing seemed the same, especially when people start rumors that her father had stolen money from a client, Mr. Carrington.

Jodie knows her father wasn't the thief. Jodie and her family are invited to spend Christmas at East Hill. East Hill was where Jodie grew up and where her Aunt Winifred lives. Her mother and brother decide not to go, but Jodie chooses to go in hopes of finding the real thief.

When Jodie arrives at Aunt Winifred's big house, she decides to play detective and look for clues. And when she looks in the attic, some big secrets are revealed! Yes, I liked the book. Yes, I thought it was interesting. I would definitely recommend it because it was very scary. Yes, you will love it.

**Noelle Salese, Grade 5
Bronx, New York**

Dead Wrong

by Alida E. Young

128 pages

Let me tell you about the gripping book I read. In *Dead Wrong,* a girl named Staci has a big brother named Matt. Matt takes steroids to get big and strong just so he can win a scholarship. Steroids are a kind of drug. Read this book to find out a terrible thing that happens to Matt and his sister.

This book teaches you not to use drugs. I like this book because it made me realize we can win, maybe not a scholarship, but life.

**Bonita Hernandez, Grade 5
Colorado Springs, Colorado**

Shared Reading

There's nothing like a great book—except sharing it! Here's how:

1. **Read aloud.** Make it part of your family's daily routine.
2. **Start a book discussion group.** Ask a librarian or teacher to help.
3. **Read to someone who can't.** Check out *The Kid's Guide to Service Projects* by Barbara Lewis to find an audience who will appreciate a reader.

Save My Rainforest

by Monica Zak

29 pages

Save My Rainforest is a great book. It's about a boy who wants to save the last rainforest in Mexico. Can you believe, he waits for four days at the president's house just to talk to him? Well it's true! He and his father also walk all the way to the rainforest, and on the way, they camp by the side of the road. This is a true story of a boy who is determined to save the last rainforest. There is a lot more to know about this story, but you'll find that out when you read it.

Raquel Vechinski, Grade 5
Wisconsin Rapids, Wisconsin

Tropical Trivia

Rain forests cover only 6 percent of the earth, but they contain more than half the earth's species—and affect the health of others around the world. Many medicines, foods, and spices have come from tropical rain forests. Unfortunately, the loss of rain forests, cleared for farmland or logging, causes several species to become extinct *every day!*

A Young Painter: The Life and Paintings of Wang Yani—China's Extraordinary Young Artist

by Zheng Zhensun and Alice Low

80 pages

Boy, have I got something to tell you about! I just finished a great book. It's called *A Young Painter*. It is about an extraordinarily talented young artist from China. This is the true story of a girl named Wang Yani who likes to paint. She likes painting cats, birds, and especially monkeys. The illustrations in this book include photographs of Yani and her work.

I liked this book because it tells about Wang Yani, how she paints, the tools and materials she uses, her life in China, and the reason she paints. I also liked reading about an artist who started drawing at age two, just like me. I give this book two thumbs-up!

Melissa Fritsch, Grade 3
Lynnwood, Washington

Your Turn: How to Write a Review

Did you agree with the reviews you read? People react to books in different ways. Now it's your turn to write your own reviews. Here are questions that will help you get started. Pick at least four questions to answer in your review and check them off. (We've checked off the first one to get you started.) Use the next page to write your review. Don't forget to fill in the genre and write an interesting tidbit for the Extra! feature. Collect a group of reviews from your friends and classmates and put them together for your own edition of *Kids Review Kids' Books*.

- ☑ What is the title of the book and the author's name?

- ☐ Would you recommend this book to others?

- ☐ Why did you like (or dislike) the main character?

- ☐ If there is artwork, did you like it? Why or why not?

- ☐ What would you change in this book? Why?

- ☐ What facts or fun things did you learn from this book?

- ☐ What did the book help you learn about yourself or someone else?

- ☐ Did the characters in the book remind you of yourself or anyone else? Why?

- ☐ Did this book remind you of any other books? Which ones, and why?

- ☐ Did the book leave you with something to think about? What?

(If you have other questions write them here.)

_____

_____

_____

▼ **Title** _____

▼ **Author** _____

▼ **Genre** _____ ▼ **Pages** _____

▼ **Review** _____

_____

_____

_____

_____

_____

_____

_____

_____

▼ **Reviewed by** _____ ▼ **Grade** _____

▼ **School** _____

▼ **City, State** _____

▼ **Extra!** _____

_____

_____

_____

▼ **Meet the Reviewer!** _____

_____

_____

_____

Title Index

How to Use the Title Index: To find a review on a specific book, look under the letter the book begins with. Find out the author's last name, then use the letter it begins with to locate the review. The reviews are arranged in alphabetical order according to the authors' last names.

A

Ace, the Very Important Pig by Dick King-Smith

The Adventures of Ratman by Ellen Weiss and Mel Friedman

The Adventures of Tom Sawyer by Mark Twain

Aliens for Breakfast by Jonathan Etra and Stephanie Spinner

All the Days of Her Life by Lurlene McDaniel

Amazing Grace by Mary Hoffman

Amber Brown Is Not a Crayon by Paula Danzinger

Amelia Earhart: Adventure in the Sky by Francene Sabin

America's Children selected by Linda Etkin and Bebe Willoughby

Anne Frank: The Diary of a Young Girl by Anne Frank

Anne of Green Gables by L. M. Montgomery

Are You There, God? It's Me, Margaret by Judy Blume

Attaboy, Sam! by Lois Lowry

B

Babushka's Doll by Patricia Polacco

Baby by Patricia MacLachlan

Baby Alicia Is Dying by Lurlene McDaniel

Back Home by Michelle Magorian

Bad Dreams by R. L. Stine

Baseball Saved Us by Ken Mochizuki

The Battle for the Castle by Elizabeth Winthrop

Beezus and Ramona by Beverly Cleary

Betsy and Tacy Go Over the Big Hill by Maud Hart Lovelace

Between Two Worlds by Candice Ransom

The B.F.G. by Roald Dahl

Big for Christmas by Francine Pascal

Black Beauty by Anna Sewell

Black Star, Bright Dawn by Scott O'Dell

Boonsville Bombers by Alison C. Herzig

The Borderline Case by Franklin W. Dixon

Borreguita and the Coyote by Verna Aardema

The Borrowers by Mary Norton

Bridge to Terabithia by Katherine Paterson

Brighty of the Grand Canyon by Marguerite Henry

Bunnicula: A Rabbit Tale of Mystery by James Howe

Bury My Bones, But Keep My Words: African Tales for Retelling retold by Tony Fairman

C

Cajun Night Before Christmas by "Trosclair"

California Girls by Ann M. Martin

Call It Courage by Armstrong Sperry

The Call of the Wild by Jack London

Cam Jansen and the Mystery of the Monster Movie by David A. Adler

The Camp-Out Mystery by Gertrude Chandler Warner

Carry On, Mr. Bowditch by Jean Lee Latham

The Cat Who Went to Heaven by Elizabeth Coatsworth

Catherine, Called Birdy by Karen Cushman

Catwings by Ursula K. LeGuin

Charlie and the Chocolate Factory by Roald Dahl

Charlotte's Web by E. B. White

Cheetahs, the Swift Hunters by Gladys Conklin

Chicken Sunday by Patricia Polacco

The Chronicles of Narnia by C. S. Lewis

Cloudy With a Chance of Meatballs by Judi Barrett

The Computer That Ate My Brother by Dean Marney

The Courage of Sarah Noble by Alice Dalgliesh

Cousins by Virginia Hamilton

Crystal by Walter Dean Myers

D

Daniel's Story by Carol Matas

Danny, the Champion of the World by Roald Dahl

Dead Wrong by Alida E. Young

Dinosaur Discoveries: How to Create Your Own Prehistoric World by Robin West

Dinotopia by James Gurney

Dolphin Adventure: A True Story by Wayne Grover

Don't Hurt Laurie! by Willo Davis Roberts

Doodle Soup by John Ciardi

E

Elaine and the Flying Frog by Heidi Chang

Eleanor Roosevelt: First Lady of the World by Doris Faber

Emily by Michael Bedard

Encyclopedia Brown and the Case of the Dead Eagles by Donald J. Sobol

Esio Trot by Roald Dahl

Extremely Weird Frogs by Sarah Lovett

Eye Magic: Fantastic Optical Illusions—An Interactive Pop-up Book by Sarah Hewetson

The Eyes of the Killer Robot by John Bellairs

F

The Face on the Milk Carton by Caroline B. Cooney

Family Pictures by Carmen Lomas Garza

The Family Under the Bridge by Natalie Savage Carlson

Farmer Boy by Laura Ingalls Wilder

Ferret in the Bedroom, Lizards in the Fridge by Bill Wallace

The Flying Tortoise retold by Tololwa M. Mollel

Forward Pass by Thomas J. Dygard

Freckle Juice by Judy Blume

Frederick Douglass Fights for Freedom by Margaret Davidson

Friedrich by Hans Peter Richter

From the Mixed-up Files of Mrs. Basil E. Frankweiler by E. L. Konigsburg

Fudge-a-Mania by Judy Blume

G

George Washington's Socks by Elvira Woodruff

Ghost Hotel by Larry Weinberg

The Ghost Ship Mystery by Gertrude Chandler Warner

Ghosts in Fourth Grade by Constance Hiser

Gift Horse by Virginia Vail

The Giraffe and the Pelly and Me by Roald Dahl

The Giver by Lois Lowry

The Giving Tree by Shel Silverstein

Glass Slippers Give You Blisters by Mary Jane Auch

Go Eat Worms! by R. L. Stine

Goblins in the Castle by Bruce Coville

The Gold Coin by Alma F. Ada

The Golden Days by Gail Radley

Gone-Away Lake by Elizabeth Enright

Good Night, Mr. Tom by Michelle Magorian

Grandfather's Journey by Allen Say

The Great Barrier Reef: A Living Laboratory by Rebecca L. Johnson

The Great Gilly Hopkins by Katherine Paterson

Gross Facts to Blow Your Mind by Judith Freeman Clark and Stephen Long

Gwinna by Barbara Helen Berger

H

Hangman by John Peel

Hard Drive to Short by Matt Christopher

Harriet the Spy by Louise Fitzhugh

Harriet Tubman: The Road to Freedom by Rae Bains

Hatchet by Gary Paulsen

The Haunted House by Francine Pascal

The Haunted Mask by R. L. Stine

Helen Keller by Margaret Davidson

Here Comes Zelda Claus by Lynn Hall

Here's to You, Rachel Robinson by Judy Blume

The Heroine of the Titanic: A Tale Both True and Otherwise of the Life of Molly Brown by Joan W. Blos

The Hobbit by J. R. R. Tolkien

Home for the Howl-idays by Dian Curtis Reagan

The Home Run Kings by Clare and Frank Gault

How Did We Find Out the Earth Is Round? by Isaac Asimov

How to Eat Fried Worms by Thomas Rockwell

Hut School and the Wartime Home Front Heroes by Robert Burch

I

I Hate English! by Ellen Levine

I, Houdini: The Autobiography of a Self-Educated Hamster by Lynne Reid Banks

I Want to Live by Lurlene McDaniel

The Ice Princess by Nicholas Walker

Ida Early Comes Over the Mountain by Robert Burch

If You Want to Scare Yourself by Angela Sommer-Bodenburg

If You're Not Here, Please Raise Your Hand: Poems About School by Kalli Dakos

I'll Always Love You by Hans Wilhelm

In the Year of the Boar and Jackie Robinson by Betty Bao Lord

The Incredible Journey by Sheila Burnford

The Indian in the Cupboard by Lynne Reid Banks

Indian Summer by Barbara Girion

Indiana Jones and the Cult of the Mummy's Crypt by R. L. Stine

Inside Dinosaurs and Other Prehistoric Creatures by Stephen Parker

Invisible Bugs and Other Creepy Creatures That Live With You by Susan S. Lang

Island of the Blue Dolphins by Scott O'Dell

The Island on Bird Street by Uri Orlev

It's Not the End of the World by Judy Blume

J

The Jack-O'-Lantern That Ate My Brother by Dean Marney

Jacob's Rescue, A Holocaust Story by Malka Drucker and Michael Halperin

James and the Giant Peach by Roald Dahl

Jessi's Secret Language by Ann M. Martin

Jim Abbott by John Rolfe

Joe Montana by Marc Appleman

The Jolly Man by Jimmy Buffet and Savannah Jane Buffett

Journey to Jo'burg: A South African Story by Beverly Naidoo

A Journey to the Centre of the Earth by Jules Verne

Julian, Secret Agent by Ann Cameron

Julie by Jean Craighead George

Jumanji by Chris Van Allsburg

June 29, 1999 by David Wiesner

Jurassic Park: The Junior Novelization screenplay by Michael Crichton and David Koepp, adapted by Gail Herman

Just as Long as We're Together by Judy Blume

Justin and the Best Biscuits in the World by Mildred Pitts Walter

K

Karen's Toothache by Ann M. Martin

Kate's Turn by Jeanne Betancourt

The Kid Who Only Hit Homers by Matt Christopher

Kings, Gods and Spirits from African Mythology by Jan Knappert

Kirsten Learns a Lesson: A School Story by Janet Shaw

Knights of the Kitchen Table by John Scieszka

Knots on a Counting Rope by Bill Martin, Jr., and John Archambault

Koala by Caroline Arnold

Koi and the Kola Nuts by Brian Gleeson

Kristy and the Missing Child by Ann M. Martin

L

The Land of Gray Wolf by Thomas Locker

The Legend of Jimmy Spoon by Kristiana Gregory

Let the Circle Be Unbroken by Mildred D. Taylor

Letters From a Slave Girl: The Story of Hariet Jacobs by Mary E. Lyons

Letters From Rifka by Karen Hesse

Lift Every Voice and Sing by James Weldon Johnson

A Light in the Attic by Shel Silverstein

The Lion, the Witch and the Wardrobe by C. S. Lewis

A Little Bit Dead by Chap Reaver

Little House in the Big Woods by Laura Ingalls Wilder

Little House on Rocky Ridge by Roger Lea MacBride

Little House on the Prairie by Laura Ingalls Wilder

The Little Island by Golden MacDonald

Little Sister by Kathleen Daly

Little Women by Louisa May Alcott

Lives of the Musicians: Good Times, Bad Times (And What the Neighbors Thought) by Kathleen Krull

Lizard Music by D. Manus Pinkwater

Long Meg by Rosemary Minard

The Lost Locket by Carol Matas

Lost on a Mountain in Maine by Donn Fendler

M

The Magic Amber retold by Charles Reasoner

The Magic School Bus Inside the Earth by Joanna Cole

The Magician's Nephew by C. S. Lewis

Mama, Let's Dance by Patricia Hermes

Maniac Magee by Jerry Spinelli

Martin Luther King, Jr.: Free at Last by David A. Adler

Mary Anne and the Secret in the Attic by Ann M. Martin

The Math Wiz by Betsy Duffey

Matilda by Roald Dahl

Medical Mysteries: Six Deadly Cases by Dian Dincin Buchman

Meet Addy by Connie Porter

Meet Kirsten: An American Girl by Janet Shaw

Meet Samantha by Susan S. Adler

Merry Christmas, Amelia Bedelia by Peggy Parish

The Midnight Club by Christopher Pike

Miracle at the Plate by Matt Christopher

Moby-Dick by Herman Melville, adapted by Patricia Daniels

Molly's Pilgrim by Barbara Cohen

Monkey Island by Paula Fox

The Monument by Gary Paulsen

Morning Girl by Michael Dorris

Mostly Michael by Robert Kimmel Smith

The Mouse and the Motorcycle by Beverly Cleary

Mozart: Scenes from the Childhood of the Great Composer by Catherine Brighton

Mr. Popper's Penguins by Richard and Florence Atwater

Muggie Maggie by Beverly Cleary

My Babysitter Has Fangs by Ann Hodgman

My Brother Sam Is Dead by James L. Collier and Christopher Collier

My Dad Lives in a Downtown Hotel by Peggy Mann

My Hairiest Adventure by R. L. Stine

My Side of the Mountain by Jean Craighead George

My Teacher Fried My Brains by Bruce Coville

My Teacher Is an Alien by Bruce Coville

The Mystery of Chimney Rock by Edward Packard

The Mystery of the Cupboard by Lynne Reid Banks

Stealing Home: The Story of Jackie Robinson by Barry Denenberg

The Stinky Cheese Man and Other Fairly Stupid Tales by Jon Scieszka and Lane Smith

Stone Fox by John Reynolds Gardiner

Stonewords: A Ghost Story by Pam Conrad

Storms by Seymour Simon

A Story, A Story by Gail E. Haley

The Story of the White House by Kate Waters

Streams to the River, River to the Sea by Scott O'Dell

Striped Ice Cream by Joan M. Lexau

Stuart Little by E. B. White

Sugar Isn't Everything by Willo Davis Roberts

The Summer of the Swans by Betsy Byars

A Summer to Die by Lois Lowry

Superfudge by Judy Blume

The Swiss Family Robinson by Johann David Wyss

T

Tales of a Fourth Grade Nothing by Judy Blume

A Taste of Blackberries by Doris Buchanan Smith

Teammates by Peter Golenbock

Teeth Week by Nancy Alberts

Ten Great Mysteries by Edgar Allan Poe

The Terrible Turnoff and Me by Joan Thompson

The Terrible Wave by Marden Dahlstedt

Thank You, Jackie Robinson by Barbara Cohen

There's a Boy in the Girls' Bathroom by Louis Sachar

There's a Girl in My Hammerlock by Jerry Spinelli

Thirteen edited by Tonya Pines

This Is My House by Arthur Dorros

The Three Little Javelinas by Susan Lowell

Three of a Kind by Louise Rich

Thunder Cake by Patricia Polacco

Tiger Eyes by Judy Blume

Tituba of Salem Village by Ann Petry

To Kill a Mockingbird by Harper Lee

To Space and Back by Sally Ride with Susan Okie

Too Young to Die by Lurlene McDaniel

Trail of Apple Blossoms by Irene Hunt

Treasure Mountain by Evelyn Sibley Lampman

The True Confessions of Charlotte Doyle by Avi

The Trumpet of the Swan by E. B. White

Turn Homeward, Hannalee by Patricia Beatty

The Twenty-One Balloons by William Pene DuBois

Two Old Women: An Alaskan Legend of Betrayal, Courage and Survival by Velma Wallis

U

Undying Glory: The Story of the Massachusetts 54th Regiment by Clinton Cox

Unfinished Portrait of Jessica by Richard Peck

Up From Slavery by Booker T. Washington

W

Waitress by D. Smith

Walking the Road to Freedom: A Story About Sojourner Truth by Jeri Ferris

Wanted . . . Mud Blossom by Betsy Byars

The War With Grandpa by Robert Kimmel Smith

The Westing Game by Ellen Raskin

What the Witch Left by Ruth Chew

When I Was Young in the Mountains by Cynthia Rylant

Where the Bald Eagles Gather by Dorothy H. Patent

Where the Red Fern Grows by Wilson Rawls

Where the Sidewalk Ends by Shel Silverstein

The Whipping Boy by Sid Fleischman

White Fang II: Myths of the White Wolf by Elizabeth Faucher

Who Comes with Cannons? by Patricia Beatty

Who Let Girls in the Boys' Locker Room? by Elaine Moore

The Wild Culpepper Cruise by Gary Paulsen

Wild Weather: Tornadoes! by Lorraine Jean Hopping

William and Boomer by Lindsay Barrett George

The Witches by Roald Dahl

The World's Best Jinx McGee by Katherine Applegate

The Wreck of the Zephyr by Chris Van Allsburg

The Wright Brothers at Kitty Hawk by Donald J. Sobol

A Wrinkle in Time by Madeleine L'Engle

Y

You Shouldn't Have To Say Good-bye by Patricia Hermes

A Young Painter: The Life and Paintings of Wang Yani—China's Extraordinary Young Artist by Zheng Zhensun and Alice Low

Your Best Friend, Kate by Pat Brisson

Z

Zlata's Diary: A Child's Life in Sarajevo by Zlata Filipovic